Published in the United Kingdom by
Ptarmigan Publishing Ltd
46 New Park Street Devizes Wiltshire SN10 1DT

Telephone	+44 (0)1380 728700
Facsimile	+44 (0)1380 728701
E mail	enquiries@distinctionworld.com
Web site	**www.distinctionworld.com**

Production & editorial director	**Mark Dawson**
Sales manager	**Susan Parker**
Administrator	**Kate Mousley**
Publisher & managing director	**Mark Hodson**

Colour origination and print:
Butler & Tanner Limited, Frome.

© Ptarmigan Publishing Ltd 2001

ISBN 1 904122 00 0

British Library Cataloguing in Publication Data. A catalogue record for this book is available from the British Library.

Photograph 'The Chefs' courtesy of Longueville Manor
Photograph 'The Recipes' courtesy of Sheen Falls Lodge

CHEFS OF
Distinction
VOLUME TWO

EDITED BY

JANE PRUDEN

The King and I

HISTORY IN A GLASS

Serena Sutcliffe, MW discovers the personalities and the history behind one of the world's most illustrious châteaux – Haut-Brion.

Drinking a wine that has been praised by Samuel Pepys, John Locke and John Evelyn gives an extra frisson at the best of times, but when that wine is also immeasurably sumptuous, one approaches paradise. Certainly, I shall never get any nearer! This short-cut to the stars is accomplished by acquiring a bottle of Château Haut-Brion – never mind the vintage, they are all good, although some are extra-terrestrial.

How is greatness in a wine achieved? There are certain given prerequisites, such as perfect 'terroir' – a seemingly mysterious word that encapsulates ideal soil, site and micro-climate. Haut-Brion has all of these, plus inspired ownership and management. The human element is vital in the creation of a great wine, since decisions affecting the quantity to be produced – such as pruning tightly, 'dropping' some of the crop and deciding on the proportion of wine that goes into the 'grand vin' – are both strategic and financial, often involving costly sacrifices. The difference between a very good and a great wine is, to a large extent, due to an accumulation of little details, and this needs leadership, vigilance and a common aim. These details include the gentleness of the press used, fermentation temperatures, the type of fertiliser in the vineyard, when old vines are pulled up and new ones planted, the timing of the picking and bottling, the treatment of the oak in the barrels – to name just a few 'flash factors'.

The Château Haut-Brion estate was first established by the de Pontac family in the 16th century and, in the 17th century, Haut-Brion became the first wine to be sold under the name of its vineyard site – it was as fashionable in the London eating-houses of the epoch as Hildon Water is today. By the mid-18th century, the wine was being bottled at the château, which was very advanced for the time. In 1855, Haut-Brion was named as one of the original First Growths in the famous Bordeaux classification of the top châteaux and, as a Graves, it was the only non-Médoc wine in the classification. In 1935, the estate was acquired by the American, Clarence Dillon, and, since then, it has remained in the same family ownership.

Now, the son of the Duchesse de Mouchy (née Joan Dillon), Prince Robert of Luxembourg, has taken over the management and there is no doubt that this continuity has been enormously beneficial to Haut-Brion, particularly since the family is so dedicated to quality. The property has also had the unique advantage of a parallel family on the wine-making side. Jean-Bernard Delmas took over from his father as régisseur in 1961, making him the doyen of all First Growth technical directors. His professional integrity and keen mind have resulted in an extraordinary run of great Haut-Brions and his pioneering work on clones with the National Agricultural Research Institute has benefited all Bordeaux.

What is the essence of the smell and taste of Haut-Brion? The flavour of Pessac, in the northern part of the Graves, is epitomised in Châteaux Haut-Brion, La Mission Haut-Brion (also owned since 1983 by Domaine Clarence Dillon) and Pape-Clément, but the fascinating thing (which keeps us all enthralled by fine wine) is that they are all completely different.

A common denominator can be a similarity with caramelised black fruit jam at the bottom of a pan! Havana cigars on the bouquet is another recognisable trait. Coffee and caramel are often there, but the Haut-Brion special can be a characteristic aftertaste of cold coffee – amazingly recognisable once you are alerted to it. The smokiness you often find in Haut-Brion is not from over-toasting of the casks (it can even appear in the wine while it is in vat!) – it is the wine itself. Recent tastings have shown that, in certain years, Haut-Brion has a magnificent peatiness to it, reminiscent of the very best Islay Malt. This really appeals to the Scottish side of me – as if I were not already passionate enough about this wine. Haut-Brion is extraordinarily voluptuous and more-ish; welcoming, complex and wrap-around enveloping. It is the First Growth to sink into – let yourself be seduced and beguiled by it.

The vintages of Haut-Brion that are drinking really well at the moment are 1993 and 1994, neither of which will break the bank in First Growth terms. Younger vintages still need keeping – 1997 less so than 1995/1996, and certainly less than the great trio 1998, 1999 and 2000. This March, it was palpably exciting to taste the 2000 in cask, with its whiff of sandalwood and great freshness and vivacity – a hallmark of this much-lauded year.

If you frequent the auction saleroom, you will still be able to buy another superb trio of Haut-Brions – 1990, 1989 (judged to be the wine of the entire vintage) and 1988 – as well as 1986, 1985, 1983 and 1982, all textbook examples of the château. Should you wish to buy the 1979, however, you might find yourself bidding against the owner, Prince Robert, as it is a personal favourite of his!

THE CHEFS

THE RECIPES

THE SAVOY

Anton Edelmann

Seared king scallops on lobster succotash

serves 4

8 King scallops, washed and dried

¹/2 lemon, juiced

1 x 800g lobster, boiled for 6 minutes, shells removed and cut into 1 cm pieces

1 shallot, peeled and finely chopped

¹/2 garlic clove, peeled and crushed

1 red chilli, inside removed and finely chopped

50g leek, cut into ¹/2cm pieces and washed

100ml white wine

200ml double cream

50g sweet corn kernels

50g diced tomatoes, blanched and peeled

50g broad beans, blanched and peeled

olive oil

salt and freshly ground pepper

for the red pepper coulis

4 medium red peppers

60g unsalted butter, chilled and diced

salt and freshly ground pepper

for the lemon dressing

30ml olive oil

10ml lemon juice

salt and pepper

4 spring onions, cut into julienne strips

2 sweet carrots, cut into julienne strips

6 radishes, cut into julienne strips

freshly picked flat parsley or coriander leaves

Sweat the shallots in oil, until they become translucent. Add the chilli, garlic, and sweat for a further minute. Add the leek and sweat slowly until soft. Add the white wine and reduce. Add the double cream and reduce further until slightly thickened. For the American succotash, add the sweet corn kernels, tomatoes, broad beans and then the lobster pieces and season with salt and pepper.

Heat a little olive oil in a non-stick pan, season the scallops and fry quickly on both sides. Pour the excess oil away. Add the lemon juice and cook the scallops quickly until all the juice has reduced and caramelised.

To make the red pepper coulis, cut the peppers in half and remove the core and seeds. Roughly chop the peppers and place in a food processor. Pulse to a fairly smooth purée and pass through a fine sieve lined with muslin. Squeeze out the muslin to extract any further juice. Pour the liquid into a saucepan and reduce by a generous half by boiling fast. Allow to cool slightly, then whisk in the butter a little at a time to thicken and enrich the sauce. Adjust seasoning to taste.

To serve, arrange some lobster succotash on the plates with the scallops and pour a little red pepper coulis around it. Mix together the ingredients for the lemon dressing and toss into all the ingredients for the radish salad and place on top of the scallops.

Meli Melo of lamb on minted pea purée

serves 4

4 x 60g pieces of lamb cutlets

4 x 80g pieces of lamb fillets,
all skin and bones removed

4 wedges of potato cake
with lamb confit

200g mixed vegetables –
yellow/green courgette, white/green
asparagus, carrots, kohlrabi –
cut into julienne strips

olive oil

salt and black pepper mill

**for the potato cake
with lamb confit**

300g potatoes, finely sliced

7g rosemary, chopped

3g thyme, chopped

10ml olive oil

280g lamb confit

50ml chicken stock

salt and pepper

for the minted pea puree

200g frozen peas

50g onions, chopped

1 clove garlic, peeled and crushed

150ml double cream

100ml white wine

1 teaspoon mint, chopped

salt and pepper

50ml olive oil

for the Madeira sauce

40g shallots, chopped

65g unsalted butter

24 black peppercorns, crushed

1 sprig of thyme

50ml Madeira

50ml truffle juice

1 litre jus de veau
or reduced veal stock

To make the potato cake with lamb confit, slice and season the potatoes and mix with olive oil. Layer the potatoes around a dish 2-3 times with seasoning and chopped herbs. Place a thick layer of lamb confit between the final layer of potato. Cover with chicken stock and bake in the oven for 1 1/2 hours at 180°C/Gas Mark 4. When cooked, chill and press with a heavy weight.

Season the lamb with salt and pepper and turn in the oil. Grill until marks show on the meat. Place on a baking tray and cook in the oven at 200°C/Gas Mark 6, until medium rare. Toss the vegetables in butter and season.

For the minted pea puree, sweat the onions in the oil until translucent and add the garlic. Sweat for a further minute. Add the white wine and reduce by half. Add the cream and continue reducing until it coats the back of the spoon. Mix in the peas and roughly puree with a stick liquidizer. Season with salt and pepper and add the mint.

To make the Madeira sauce, sweat the shallots in 50g of the butter. Add the peppercorns, thyme, Madeira and half the truffle juice.

Reduce by two-thirds and add the jus de veau. Simmer for about 10 minutes, skimming frequently. Add the remaining truffle juice and season to taste. Pass through a sieve and stir in the remaining butter.

To serve, reheat the potato in the oven so that the top is crispy.

Arrange some minted pea puree on a plate, cut the fillet of lamb and arrange with the lamb cutlet. Place the potato cake on top.

Place the vegetables on the lamb and pour a little Madeira sauce around the dish.

Pine nut soufflé with red wine ice cream

Serves 4

**300g soft cheeses,
Quark or Philadelphia**

2 free range eggs

1 free-range egg white

30g pine nut honey

finely grated zest of 1 lemon

4 teaspoon corn flour

2 tablespoons icing sugar

200ml raspberry coulis

200ml grappa sabayon

200g red wine ice cream

mint and berries for garnish

*soft butter and caster sugar
to line the dishes*

for the raspberry coulis

500g fresh raspberries

75g icing sugar

50ml lemon juice

50g red currant jelly

for the Grappa sabayon

5 egg yolks

75g caster sugar

100ml Grappa

50ml lemon juice

50ml orange juice

for the red wine ice cream

675ml red wine

200g sugar

320g butter

6 egg yolks

2 cloves

1 cinnamon stick

1 vanilla pod

Heat the oven to 220°C/Gas Mark 7. Cover the inside of the soufflé dishes with the butter and sugar. Separate the 2 whole eggs and mix together the 2 egg yolks, cheeses, lemon zest, half the corn flour and half the icing sugar, pine nut honey and the rum. Chill for 30 minutes. In a large clean bowl, whisk the 3 egg whites to a stiff peak and add the remaining icing sugar and corn flour. Gently fold the egg white into the mixture. Pour into the soufflé dishes and bake in a roasting tin half filled with water (ie a Bain Marie) for approximately 15 minutes, until risen.

To make the raspberry coulis, place the raspberries, icing sugar and lemon juice into a bowl and puree. Pass the puree through a fine sieve, making sure all the seeds are removed. Melt the jelly and stir into the mixture.

To make the Grappa sabayon, whisk together the egg yolks, caster sugar, grappa, orange and lemon juice over boiling water to form a light, fluffy sabayon.

To make the red wine ice cream, place 500ml red wine into a saucepan and reduce with cinnamon and cloves by half. Add the remaining red wine to the red wine reduction and heat to 60°C.

Using a hand whisk, blend the butter, sugar, vanilla seeds and egg yolks. The temperature must not exceed 85°C. When the mixture has thickened slightly, place the bowl in iced water and whisk until the temperature drops to 20°C.

Either churn the ice cream in a machine or overnight in the freezer.

To serve, pour the Grappa sabayon on to a plate and pour a little coulis around. Garnish with berries and place a quenelle of red wine ice cream on the side and top with mint. Remove the soufflé from the oven and turn out of the mould, place in the middle of the sabayon and dust with icing sugar.

Trevor Brooks

Red mullet Niçoise

serves 4

4 fillets of red mullet,
170–225g each

200-300g extra fine beans, cooked in
salted boiling water for 3-5 minutes,
chilled and split in half lengthways

12 cooked baby fennel

8 small new potatoes, cooked,
peeled and kept warm

6 quail eggs, cooked for 2^1/2 minutes,
refreshed and peeled

3 ripe plum tomatoes, skinned,
de-seeded and cut into 5mm dice

4 red radishes thinly sliced

1 tablespoon extra virgin olive oil

a squeeze of lemon juice

salt and pepper

for the sauce vierge

4 shallots, peeled and sliced

1 tablespoon coriander seed,
roasted and ground into powder

300ml of extra virgin olive oil

a squeeze of lemon juice

1 tablespoon basil leaves,
cut into julienne strips

1 tablespoon coriander leaves,
cut into julienne strips

salt and pepper

12 stoned black olives

To make the sauce vierge, put the
shallots, coriander seeds and olive oil
in a Pyrex bowl and keep in a warm
place to infuse for 4 hours, and then
strain through a fine sieve. Keeping
slightly warm, add the tomato dice,
basil and coriander leaves, lemon
juice, olives, salt and pepper.

Heat the olive oil in a non-stick
pan and sauté the fillets of red
mullet, skin side down for 2 minutes.
Turn over and remove the pan from
the heat. Season with lemon juice,
salt and pepper.

To serve, dress the beans with a
little sauce vierge and place in the
centre of the plates. Put a fillet of
mullet on top. Halve the eggs and
place 3 halves around the fish along
with sliced potatoes, radishes and
baby fennel. Spoon any remaining
sauce vierge around the mullet.

Saddle of roe deer with pumpkin tortellini and red cabbage

serves 4

800-900g trimmed roe deer saddle, keep trimmings for the sauce

a little oil and butter

coarsely ground black pepper

fleur de sel or Maldon sea salt

for the pasta

250g Italian flour

8-9 egg yolks

for the filling

250g pumpkin, cut into dice

2 shallots, finely chopped

$^1/_2$ clove garlic, crushed

1 tablespoon olive oil

ground white pepper

fleur de sel or Maldon sea salt

for the sauce

1 small carrot, chopped

$^1/_2$ stick celery, chopped

1 shallot, chopped

4 juniper berries, crushed

a sprig of thyme

1 tablespoon raspberry vinegar

300ml red wine

150ml port

250ml chicken stock

150ml reduced veal stock

10g ice cold butter

5-10g bitter 70% chocolate

fleur de sel Maldon sea salt

6 peppercorns, crushed

for the cabbage

$^1/_2$ a red cabbage

1 green apple peeled and sliced

1 tablespoon red wine vinegar

1-2 tablespoons brown sugar

1 rasher streaky bacon

fleur de sel or Maldon sea salt

ground black pepper

grated nutmeg

butter

First make the pasta, mixing all the ingredients in a food processor until a dough is formed. Wrap in cling film and chill until required.

Quarter and core the cabbage and cut into fine julienne strips. Melt the butter in a dish; add the cabbage and sprinkle with vinegar and grated nutmeg. Add the bacon, cover and cook gently in a moderate oven. When 3/4 cooked, add the apple and brown sugar and continue cooking very carefully. Season to taste.

For the filling, heat some oil in a pan and sweat the shallots without colour. Add the garlic and cook for 1 minute. Add the pumpkin dice and cover. Cook over a low heat until the pumpkin is very tender, pass through a fine sieve and season.

For the sauce, heat some oil in a pan; add the carrot, celery, shallot, thyme and juniper. Add the venison trimmings and cook until well browned. Drain off the oil, moisten with vinegar and de-glaze with wine and port and reduce by 3/4. Add the chicken and veal stock, bring to the

boil and skim. Reduce the heat and cook slowly for 1 hour, with the lid on.

Remove the lid, season with salt and add the peppercorns. Cook for 5 minutes and strain through a fine muslin. Whisk in the butter and chocolate. Taste and adjust the seasoning if necessary.

Roll out the pasta as thinly as possible and cut out 12 x 6cm circles. Place a teaspoon of the purée in the centre and moisten the edges with water and fold over into a semi-circle. Wrap around your little finger and seal the points together with a little water.

To cook the saddle of roe deer, heat the oil and butter in a heavy frying pan. Lightly season the saddle and fry briskly until coloured on both sides in the oil and butter. Place in a hot oven for 4-6 minutes. Remove and allow to rest in a warm place for 10 minutes. Cut into 4 pieces and sprinkle with salt and coarsely ground black pepper.

To serve, cook the tortellini pasta in boiling salted water for 3-4 minutes, drain and keep warm. Spoon the red cabbage on to the centre of the plates and place the venison on top. Arrange the tortellini around the plates and spoon over the sauce.

Millefeuille of meringue biscuits
with passion fruit mousse and exotic fruits

serves 4

for the meringues

4 egg whites

115g granulated sugar

115g icing sugar

2 teaspoons of poppy seeds

for the mousse

400ml passion fruit purée

4 egg yolks

40g flour, sieved

250ml whipping cream

for the vanilla, mint and lime syrup

250g granulated sugar

100ml water

1 vanilla pod, split and de-seeded

1 star anise

juice of 1 lime

for the exotic fruits

1 mango

1 kiwi fruit

2 figs

2 passion fruit

1 ugli fruit

1 banana

1 lime zest, cut into julienne strips

a handful of mint leaves

For the meringues, start by making an 8cm circular template from an old plastic lid. Whisk the egg whites with granulated sugar for 5 minutes. Gently fold in sieved icing sugar and use immediately. Line a baking sheet with silicon paper and using the template, make 12 discs of meringue. Sprinkle 4 of the discs with poppy seeds. Bake in a low oven at approximately 100°C/Gas Mark 1/2 until dry and crisp. Remove and cool.

To make the mousse, whisk the egg yolks, sugar and flour together. Whisk the purée into the yolk mixture. Put into a heavy based saucepan, over a low heat and slowly bring to the boil, mixing all the time until the mixture thickens.

Pass through a sieve, cool and chill in the fridge. Whip the cream and fold into the passion fruit mixture.

Place all the ingredients for the syrup into a pan and bring to the boil. Leave to infuse for 1 hour and strain.

Peel and cut the exotic fruit into attractive shapes and blanch the lime zest.

To serve, place a meringue biscuit, in the centre of each plate. Put a spoonful of mousse on the biscuit. Top with a second meringue biscuit and put another spoonful of mousse on top of that. Finish with a poppy seed meringue. Arrange the fruits and lime zest around the millefeuille, drizzle with syrup and garnish with mint leaves.

DROMOLAND CASTLE

David McCann

Ravioli of scallops with basil and tomato, citrus sauce

serves 4

for the pasta

200g strong flour

1 whole egg

2 yolks

2 tablespoons of extra virgin olive oil

pinch of salt

for the filling

4 scallops, orange tongue removed

100g John Dory flesh

1 egg white

100ml double cream

salt and pepper for seasoning

for the sauce

1 orange zest and juice

1 lime zest and juice

1 lemon zest and juice

2 shallots, diced

1 clove garlic

pinch of saffron

50ml of white wine

50ml of Noilly Pratt

1 sprig of basil

200ml mussel and scallop stock

seasoning

for the garnish

baby spinach

1 tomato, skinned and diced

4 scallops

chopped chives

Place the sieved flour and salt in a bowl and add the beaten egg, yolk and oil. Mix to form a dough. Cover and rest for 1 hour. Using a pasta machine, roll out the dough and gradually reduce to the finest setting. Cut 8 x 8cm discs.

Remove the scallops from their shells and reserve the orange tongues for later. In a food processor, blend the white scallop meat and John Dory until smooth and add the egg white. Blend and then slowly add the double cream. Season with salt and pepper and pass the filling through a fine sieve. Dice the tongues and add to the filling.

Evenly place half of the ravioli mix on each of the 4 pasta discs. Egg-wash the rims, place the 4 other discs on top and seal the edges. Cook in boiling salted water for 2 minutes, drain and reserve.

To make the sauce, sweat the zest and shallots, add all the other ingredients, except the cream and butter. Reduce to a syrup, add the cream and bring to the boil and simmer until correct consistency. Pass through a fine sieve. Correct the seasoning and whisk in the unsalted butter and juice.

To serve, sauté 4 whole scallops. In a separate pan, sauté the baby spinach then add butter and season. Warm the tomato dice. Place the spinach in a pasta bowl, ravioli on top followed by the tomato and scallop. Whisk the sauce until light and drizzle over the ravioli and sprinkle with chives.

Pan-fried fillet of sea bass with buttered pak choi, Nice olives, red pepper and courgettes

serves 4

8 x 80g pieces of filleted sea bass

40g Nice olive purée

1 clove garlic

2 medium red bell peppers, blanched and diced

4 medium tomatoes, skinned and diced

5 small heads of pak choi

3 large courgettes

3 large shallots

basil

extra virgin olive oil

100ml white wine

400ml shellfish and fish stock

1 dash sherry vinegar

mixed chopped herbs, parsley, tarragon, chives, basil, dill and chervil

Wash the courgettes, drain and dry. Cut into copeaux, (round pieces of courgette, skin-side on top). To cook, sauté in olive oil, season and drain. Wash the pak choi, remove the root end and break up into small pieces. To cook, sauté lightly in olive oil with a hint of garlic and season.

Place the wine and stock in a saucepan and reduce by 95%. Soften the diced shallots in olive oil, add the vinegar, the diced red pepper and lastly the reduced stock and tomato dice. Season and add the chopped herbs and leave to infuse.

Cook the sea bass in olive oil, skin side only until the fish is ready, flip over to seal and allow to rest.

To serve, place the pak choi in the centre of the plate surrounded by 6 pieces of courgette. Place 2 pieces of sea bass on top of the pak choi, garnished with olive purée and basil. Drizzle the sauce evenly around the plate.

Bitter and white chocolate truffle mousse on a hazelnut and almond base with cappuccino sabayon

serves 4

for the bitter and white chocolate mousse

50g sugar

1 egg yolk

1 whole egg

100g white chocolate

100g dark chocolate

200g whipped cream

for the hazelnut and almond base

2 egg whites

50g caster sugar

25g ground almonds

25g hazelnuts

12g plain flour

for the nougatine

100g flaked almonds

110g sugar

5g butter

to decorate

50g cocoa powder, sieved

100g melted dark chocolate

50g melted white chocolate

To make the base, whisk the egg whites and sugar until stiff. Sieve the rest of the ingredients and fold in lightly. Spread out the mixture on a flat tray on greaseproof paper, 12" x 8". Bake in a hot oven 200°C/Gas Mark 6 for 10 minutes. When cold, cut out 4 circular bases with ring moulds.

For the chocolate mousse, melt chocolates separately. Whip the cream. Whisk the egg until light and fluffy. Put the sugar on to boil with a little water to cover until 121°C. Pour liquid sugar on to whisking eggs and continue whisking until cold. Remove half the mixture. Whisk the first half into the dark chocolate then add half of the cream. Whisk the second half in the white chocolate then add the rest of the cream. Place the dark chocolate mixture onto the hazelnut and almond base in the 4 individual rings, then pour in the white chocolate mixture on top of that and allow to set for 4 hours.

For the nougatine, heat the sugar over a low heat, add heated almonds and butter and melt. Turn out onto an oiled tray and roll out and shape while still warm.

To serve, cover some greaseproof paper with melted chocolate and refrigerate. Cut out rectangles 4cm x 2cm. Dust each with icing sugar and cocoa powder alternatively and place around the de-moulded mousse. Dust the mousse with cocoa powder on top. As an option, draw out a butterfly with dark chocolate and allow to chill. Then fill with white chocolate. When chilled, place on top of the mousse. Draw a design on the plate for decoration.

THE LOWRY HOTEL

David Woolf

Drones potted shrimps with gulls eggs and caviar

serves 4

for the potted shrimps

1kg brown shrimps

250g unsalted butter

10g anchovy essence

pinch mace

pinch nutmeg

pinch cayenne pepper

splash Worcestershire sauce

lemon juice

for the brown crab mayonnaise

225g brown crabmeat

5ml Worcestershire sauce

30g egg yolks

1/2 tablespoon English mustard

1/2 tablespoon anchovy essence

60g brown breadcrumbs, crusts removed

150ml extra virgin olive oil

salt and pepper

To make the potted shrimps, soften the butter and whisk in the anchovy essence and lemon juice. Add the rest of the ingredients and fold in the shrimps. Check for seasoning.

To make the brown crab mayonnaise, put the egg yolks and the mustard in a bowl and whisk for a minute, then very slowly add the oil followed by the rest of the ingredients.

To serve, place a ring mould in the centre of each plate and fill $2/3$ with potted shrimps and top with brown crab mayonnaise. Circle with 5 small spots of crab mayonnaise and add 5 slices of gulls eggs.

Tranche of cod with clam dieppoisse, Madeira jus and dauphinoise potato

serves 6

2 fillets of cod, scaled,
pin boned with the skin left on

Maldon sea salt and pepper

for the dauphinoise potatoes

3 kg potatoes, sliced and peeled

1 litre cream

3 cloves garlic, chopped

Beaufort cheese

Gruyere cheese

salt and pepper

for the haricot blanc and clams

18 venus clams
or small palourde clams

200g haricot blanc beans,
soaked for 24 hours

1 bunch of flat leaf parsley

1 block of unsalted butter

1 carrot, halved

1 onion, halved

1 celery stick

1 bay leaf

5 peppercorns

for the Madeira jus

2 litres Madeira

2 litres veal stock

1 litres chicken stock

$^1/_2$ litre water

4 shallots, peeled and chopped

500g mushrooms, sliced

3 cloves of garlic

thyme

bay leaf

peppercorns

For the dauphinoise potatoes, reduce the cream and garlic in a pan by half. Line a large tray with greaseproof paper, then layer with sliced potatoes and a little cream and grated cheese in between. Cover with greaseproof paper and bake in the oven at 150°C/Gas Mark 2 until cooked. Chill, date and label if preparing in advance, otherwise keep warm until needed.

Take the fillets of cod, sprinkle with salt and ground white pepper and leave in the fridge for 45 minutes. The salt will have soaked into the cod firming up the flesh. Place the first fillet onto a piece of cling film skin side down and lie the other one on top, skin side up making sure that all edges are tucked in. Begin to roll inside the cling film to make a barrel. It is important at this stage to wrap the 2 fillets very tightly together, it may require two people, one to wrap and one to hold the roll of cling film. Tie the ends and rest for at least 24 hours to set.

To make the haricot blanc, firstly drain the beans and put into a pan with the vegetables and bay leaf, cover with water and add the peppercorns and some salt. Cook on a simmering heat until soft and pull all the vegetables out of the liquor and let the beans cool naturally in the pan.

Take the clams and run them under cold water for 5 minutes. Then store them in water in the fridge.

To make the Madeira jus, put a little butter and vegetable oil into a large pan and caramelise the shallots and garlic. Then add the Madeira and reduce by $^2/_3$ before adding the rest of the liquid. Add the mushrooms and the rest of the ingredients and reduce to the right consistency.

Take the cod and slice into equal pieces but leave the cling film on. Take a non-stick frying pan and add some olive oil, wait until the pan is very hot and put the cod tranches/slices in. Leave them until golden and do the same on the other side, then add a few knobs of unsalted butter to the pan and baste the cod before cooking in the oven at 180°C/Gas Mark 4 for about 6 minutes – keep basting the fish every 2 minutes.

For the haricot blanc, drain off the liquor and put into a saucepan with some light fish stock or water and a few knobs of unsalted butter. Cook the beans down into a thick emulsion and season with salt and ground white pepper, then take the parsley, pick off the stalks, cut into a fine julienne strips and add to the beans. Finally, boil the clams in fish stock and butter until they begin to open. Take them off the stove and season. Remove the clams out of the fish stock and add to the Madeira sauce.

To serve, remove any cling film and place the cod tranches/slices on top of the dauphine potato, run the beans around the outside and finish with the clams and the sauce to complete the dieppoise.

Red fruits in pink champagne jelly

serves 10

1 bottle of champagne

10ml grenadine

600g sugar

9 leaves of gelatine
soaked in very cold water

Bring the champagne and sugar to the boil in a pan. Remove from the heat and add the gelatine and grenadine, then pass through a fine sieve. Place in fridge and leave to cool for a while.

When the jelly is cool, pour about 3mms into 10 jelly moulds. Place in the fridge to set.

The red fruits used for the jelly can be a combination – it depends on preference and availability.

Once the first layer of jelly is set, place about 6 or 7 raspberries/fruits upside down. Pour in a little liquid jelly and return to the fridge to set. Be careful not to put too much jelly in or the fruit will float and the layers of jelly will be too thick. Continue with the rest of the layers making sure to set each one.

HOLBROOK HOUSE & SPA

Brett Sutton

Terrine of foie gras, baby leeks and prunes with a jelly of quince and apple, pear crisps and thyme brioche

serves 4

for the terrine

1 lobe of foie gras 'A' grade approximately 600g (available from delicatessen)

4 medium sized baby leeks

12 plump agen prunes, finely chopped

salt and pepper

150ml of chicken stock

for the quince and apple jelly

100g quince purée

100g Cox's apple purée

50-75g caster sugar

75ml water

2 1/2 leaves of gelatine

for the pear crisps

1 William pear

50g caster sugar

for the thyme brioche (makes 1 loaf)

350g of T45 flour (available from delicatessen or use strong bread flour)

1/2 teaspoon salt

15g yeast

4 tablespoon of warm milk

3 eggs, lightly beaten

175g soft unsalted butter

30g caster sugar

50g chopped fresh thyme

To make the terrine, leave the lobe of foie gras out in the kitchen for 1 hour to soften so that you can carefully remove all the veins. Then cut into 1cm wide pieces and gently pan-fry, draining any fat that comes out into a separate basin. Pan fry the foie gras for about 1 minute on either side and then place on a wire cooling rack.

Trim up the baby leeks and poach in the chicken stock for 2 minutes and leave to cool naturally.

Grease 2 small terrines and line with cling film. Next, place in 2 layers of foie gras, seasoning each layer. Then place in 2 of the well drained and dried baby leeks and a line of chopped prune either side. Then fill the terrine with the rest of the foie gras and season well.

Pour over a little of the foie gras fat that was reserved from the frying pan earlier. Fold the cling film over and press, refrigerate for 24-36 hours.

For the apple and quince jelly, place the puréed quince, apple and caster sugar in a pan. Soften the gelatine in the water. Warm the apple and quince mixture then beat in the gelatine and the water. Leave this to soak in a small tin and set for 3-6 hours.

To make the pear crisps, peel and slice very thinly by hand using a mandolin. Place the pear slices on a grease-mat and sprinkle well with the caster sugar. Cook in a low oven - 110°C/Gas Mark 1/2 for 6-8 hours.

For the thyme brioche, place the sieved flour, salt, yeast, thyme, milk and eggs into a mixer and beat on a medium speed for 5-7 minutes until it resembles elastic. Cream the butter and sugar together then gradually add this to the first mix until it becomes smooth and almost shiny. Cover with a cloth and leave to rise for 2 hours. Then knock back to the original dough size and leave to prove in the fridge overnight. Next day, grease a tin, mould and work your brioche into shape and fit into your tin. Glaze the top with an egg yolk and leave to prove again for 1-2 hours. Cook this for 10 minutes on 230°C/Gas Mark 8 and then reduce the oven to 190°C/Gas Mark 5 for a further 20-25 minutes.

Terrine of foie gras, baby leeks and prunes with a jelly of quince and apple, pear crisps and thyme brioche

Roasted fillet of beef, flaked oxtail, pomme maxime, panache of baby vegetables and cep tea sauce

Roasted fillet of beef, flaked oxtail, pomme maxime, panache of baby vegetables and cep tea sauce

serves 4

4 x 200g centre fillet of beef

1kg oxtail cut into 2" sections

for the maxime

2 large baking potatoes (Estimas)

55g butter

for the baby vegetable panache

8 baby leeks

8 baby carrots

8 baby fennel

4 baby aubergines

2 cloves of garlic

1 sprig of thyme

1 tablespoon of goose fat

4 thin slices of pancetta

for the cep tea

55g of ceps

55g mushroom trimmings

2 teabags

200ml chicken stock

100ml red wine

200ml veal stock

Firstly, braise the oxtail, sealing either side in a hot pan and then drain off the fat and place into a deep sauté or baking pan. Roast a mirepoix of root vegetables, (garlic, onion, carrot and celery) until coloured and add to the oxtail. Then deglaze the pan with red wine. Reduce this by half and then add to the oxtail. Cover with chicken stock, foil and slowly braise at 180°C/Gas Mark 4 for 4-6 hours until tender. Remove the oxtail when cooked and flake off the flesh into small chunks.

To make the pomme maxime, peel and slice the potato very thinly by hand or mandolin, cut discs about 3/4" across. You will need 15 per portion. Heat up 4 small tins. Add a little olive oil and a knob of butter, then lay the potato discs into the tin. Put each one over the next one and build to form the shape of a pinwheel, season well. Place the tin onto the stove and cook for 2-3 minutes to lightly colour, cook in the oven for 4-5 minutes. Turn out and drain off any excess fat.

For the baby vegetable panache, trim the baby leeks, blanch for 1 minute and refresh. Trim the baby fennel, blanch for 1 minute and refresh. Trim the baby carrots, blanch for 2 minutes and refresh. Confit the baby aubergines by placing them in tin foil with the goose fat, garlic and thyme. Season well and place in a medium oven for approximately 1 hour. Then to finish the panache, line the carrots, fennel and leeks up (2 of each per portion) and wrap with pancetta. Cut the aubergine from the stalk downwards, and fold this over the baby vegetables. Slowly roast together for 4-6 minutes.

For the tea, cut the ceps very finely. Add all the mushroom trimmings you have, stalks, peelings etc. Add 200ml of chicken stock, 2 tea bags and reduce the liquor down to 50ml. Add the red wine and reduce again to 50ml. Add veal stock and reduce by half. Pass through muslin.

To serve, season and seal the beef fillets in a hot pan. Cook as required and leave to rest for 5-6 minutes. Arrange the oxtail in a cutter on a plate and place the beef on the top. Place the panache of baby vegetables next to this. Let the pomme maxime lie half off the potato so it is slightly standing. The sauce should be drizzled around the plate and in between the beef and baby vegetable panache.

Assiette of mini classical British desserts

Steamed orange sponge with orange curd ice cream, rhubarb and apple crumble with cinnamon ice cream, and glazed rice pudding with butterscotch sauce

serves 4

for the glazed rice pudding

110g of carolina pudding rice, soaked in water for 1 hour

860ml milk

1 vanilla pod

110g caster sugar

30g brown sugar to glaze

for the butterscotch sauce

140g brown sugar

140g unsalted butter

255g golden syrup

260ml whipping cream

for the orange sponges

110g unsalted butter

110g caster sugar

1 egg yolk and 2 eggs (mixed)

$^1/_2$ orange zest and juice

200g self-raising flour

for the orange curd ice-cream

225g caster sugar

225g unsalted butter

4 orange zests and juice

5 egg yolks

290ml single cream

3 egg yolks

1 vanilla pod

for the rhubarb and apple crumble

1 stick of rhubarb

1 Cox's apple

50ml water

560g caster sugar

for the crumble topping

180g flour

100g Demerara sugar

100g butter

50g porridge oats

for the cinnamon ice-cream

5 egg yolks

570ml single cream

110g caster sugar

1 vanilla pod

1 cinnamon stick

To make the butterscotch sauce, put the butter, sugar and syrup into a pan. Bring to the boil and cook until golden in colour, then add cream and re-boil until thick and dark golden.

For the rice pudding, place a spoon of butterscotch sauce in the bottom of each of the 4 ramekins. Then put rinsed and drained rice into a heavy bottomed pan with milk and vanilla and cook for 10-15 minutes until tender. In a separate bowl, cream together the eggs and the sugar. Boil the rice rapidly then stir in the egg mixture and leave to cool by placing equal amounts in each ramekin. When cool and needed, sprinkle on the brown sugar and glaze under the grill or with a blowtorch.

For the orange sponges, cream the butter and sugar until white, then slowly add the egg mixture, zest and juice of the orange, then beat in the self raising flour. Mix for a further 2 minutes. Grease 4 small dariole moulds and spoon in the mixture half the way up. Cover loosely with foil and place into a roasting tin filled with water up to half way up the moulds and poach in the oven for 20-25 minutes at 190°C/Gas Mark 5.

For the orange curd ice cream, whisk the sugar and 5 yolks until light, melt the butter with the orange zest and juice. Add this all together and cook in bowl over a saucepan of water for 15 minutes until thick. Boil single cream with the vanilla pod and add to the 3 egg yolks and beat. Pass through a sieve and mix with the orange mix. Cool and place in an ice-cream machine.

To make the rhubarb and apple crumble, peel the rhubarb and the apple. Cut into 1" pieces and place into a pan with sugar and 50ml of water. Cook until soft and almost pulpy. Place equally into 4 ramekins. Rub the butter, sugar, flour and porridge oats between fingers until it becomes crumbly. Place in a layer on the top of the rhubarb mix and cook for 8-10 minutes.

To make the cinnamon ice cream, bring the vanilla, cinnamon and cream to the boil, cream the egg yolks and sugar. Add a little cream mix to the egg mixture and whisk. Then add the rest, pass through a sieve and churn in an ice-cream machine.

CHEWTON GLEN

Pierre Chevillard

Rosary goats cheese and tomato terrine

serves 8

400g Rosary goats cheese

1.25kg plum tomatoes

40ml olive oil

120g cooked beetroot

for the dressing

20ml cabernet sauvignon vinegar

10ml olive oil

salt and pepper

for the garnish

8 slices of sour bread

mixed herbs

4 slices of bacon

a handful of thyme

Blanch the tomatoes and peel, seed and quarter, reserving the seeds for the dressing. Trim the tomato slices into rectangular shapes. Line a large white china terrine with cling film. Place 1 layer of tomatoes in the bottom of the terrine followed by a second layer overlapping. Season with pepper.

Cut the goats cheese into slices about 15mm thick and layer onto the tomatoes, smoothing out all the gaps. Repeat the layering with 4 further tomato layers and 3 layers of cheese. Cover and press well. Leave overnight to chill.

To make the dressing, mix 65ml of the tomato seeds with 40ml of cabernet sauvignon vinegar and 20 ml of olive oil. Season with salt and pepper.

To serve, place 1 slice of the terrine on the plates with six slices of beetroot and drizzle dressing around. Garnish with mixed herbs. Accompany with a slice of toasted sour bread topped with sliced bacon and thyme.

Braised sea bass

serves 4

4 x 140g sea bass

240g bean sprouts

140g Shiitake mushrooms

60g ginger

120g plum tomatoes

120g spring onions

20g coriander

20g garlic

50ml Thai fish sauce

80g unsalted cooking butter

sea bass stock infused with lemon grass and ginger

Place all the raw ingredients except the tomato, butter and coriander in a dish, pour over just enough sea bass stock to cover and seal with a butter paper. Cook for approximately 5 minutes. Remove the fish from the dish and keep warm. Add butter, tomato and coriander to the ingredients remaining in the dish and heat. Adjust seasoning to taste.

Serve on a bed of sautéed pack choi.

Pineapple and marzipan savarin

serves 4

1 fresh pineapple

60g unsalted cooking butter

50ml Crème de Cacao

50g caster sugar

for the savarin/cake

125g marzipan

50g unsalted cooking butter

1 egg, separated

25g strong flour

125g caster sugar

for the pineapple crisps

remainder of the pineapple, finely sliced

100g caster sugar

250ml cold water

slice of lemon

for the decoration

4 physalis

50g sultanas

rum and raisin ice cream

For the cake, mix the marzipan with the softened butter and egg yolk. Whisk the egg with caster sugar and then fold into the egg mixture. Add flour. Put the cake mixture into 4 individually greased and lined savarin tins and bake in a moderate oven for approximately 12 minutes or until cooked.

Peel the large pineapple. Cut four 1" slices and core, retaining the remaining pineapple for decoration.

Put the caster sugar into a pan on a low heat, as it starts to dissolve add the butter and pineapple slices. Cook the pineapple on both sides in the caramel mixture. Pour over the Crème de Cacao. Retain the cooking juice.

To make the crisps, slice the remaining pineapple very thinly and place in a syrup stock made from water, sugar and the lemon slice. Allow the mixture to rest in the fridge overnight and then drain very well. Damp dry with a clean cloth or kitchen paper.

Place slices of pineapple onto a baking sheet and put into a cool oven, 85°C/Gas Mark 1/4 until dried. It is important not to shut the oven door completely as this will prevent the pineapple from drying out.

If you prefer, the pineapple wings can be made in advance and stored in an airtight container until required. When needed, they can be crisped up in the oven prior to use.

To serve, put a warm pineapple ring into the centre of each serving dish, place the cake mixture on top of the pineapple, drizzle with a little of the pineapple cooking juice. Put a scoop of the rum and raisin ice cream into the centre of each cake and place 2 of the pre-prepared pineapple wings on top. Decorate with the physalis and sultanas. Lightly dust with icing sugar.

DANESFIELD HOUSE
HOTEL & SPA

Michael Macdonald

Seared scallops, caramelised apples and Pommeau sauce

serves 4

12 similarly sized hand-dived scallops
(available from a good fishmonger)

3 Braeburn apples

400ml Pommeau aperitif

20g butter

100g sugar

selection of salad leaves

Remove the scallops from their shells, (hand-dived are preferable for their quality, but others will do just as well). Rinse and pat dry with kitchen paper and cut them in half to form discs. Peel the apples and dice into small cubes, keeping all the trimmings to one side. Melt half the butter and dissolve half the sugar in a sauté pan and caramelise the dice. Drain and repeat using the same process with the trimmings and the remaining butter and sugar as before. Liquidise the trimmings to a puréed compôte and keep separately in the fridge with the diced apples, until you are ready for assembling.

For the Pommeau sauce, reduce 300ml of the aperitif to a thick glaze and then add the remaining 100ml and continue reducing until it coats the back of a spoon.

Heat a non-stick pan with a small amount of olive oil and place the scallops cut-side down and cook until a golden brown, turn and season. Remove from the pan and keep warm.

Before assembling, warm both the compôte and the diced apples. To serve arrange a ring of dice in the centre of each plate and dot 6 even teaspoons of compôte a little way from around the edge. Then on top of the compôte, place the seared scallops cut-side up. Pile a small salad panache, seasoned with salt and olive oil on top of the diced apple and spoon the Pommeau sauce over and around the scallops.

Corn fed chicken with truffles and champagne en vessie, fresh noodles, asparagus and girolle mushrooms

serves 4

En vessie means to poach in a bag. Originally, pig's bladders were used but fortunately now we have freezer bags. This whole process ensures that the flavour of the truffle is intensified and the meat remains beautifully moist and succulent.

2 free-range corn fed chicken

2 truffles thinly sliced

500g pasta

20 baby asparagus

20 baby leeks

1 large leek

10ml olive oil

200g girolles mushrooms

2 tsp chopped herbs (chervil, chive, marjoram - mixed)

200ml champagne

for the sauce

500g chicken wings and carcass chopped small

4 shallots sliced

100g leeks finely sliced

375ml Madeira

1.14 litre of chicken stock

680ml veal stock

1 clove of garlic

thyme and 1 bay leaf

150ml cream

100ml champagne

2 tablespoons vegetable oil

for the Pasta

500g "OO" pasta flour

6 egg yolks

3 whole eggs

20ml olive oil

To make the pasta, blend all the ingredients until they come together. Remove and work by hand to a ball, then wrap and rest for 40 minutes in cling film.

Take the chicken and remove the wishbone, legs and winglets. Cut away the breasts with the skin intact from the bone. Now, working from the neck end of the breast with lightly oiled fingers so as not to tear the skin, separate the flesh from the skin to create a pocket. Oil and season the sliced truffles with olive oil and ease the mixture gently into the cavity. Season each portion and place in individual freezer bags. Pour 50ml of champagne into each bag, twist and fold the ends to expel all the air. Then place into a second freezer bag and tie, expelling the air again to finally complete the seal.

To make the sauce, caramelise the chicken bones in a pan with 2 tablespoons of vegetable oil. Remove bones and drain way all the surplus fat. Add sliced shallots and continue to caramelise adding the sliced leeks, thyme, bay leaf and garlic. Return the chicken bones back to the pan and add the Madeira. Pour in the chicken and veal stock and reduce to a glaze before adding the cream. Bring to the boil, season and strain and leave to one side.

Roll the pasta to the thinnest setting on a pasta machine and then cut into spaghetti. Rest for 10 minutes, blanch in salted water and refresh in cold water.

Cut the leeks into thin julienne strips, dry in flour and deep-fry until crisp. Add seasoning.

Submerge the chicken breasts into a pan of simmering water and cook for 15 minutes until firm to the touch.

Cook the baby leeks and baby asparagus until tender in a pan of water with a knob of butter. Sauté the girolle mushrooms and drain. Reheat the noodles and toss in butter, herbs and season to taste.

To serve, assemble the mushrooms in the middle of the plate and place a helping of noodles on the top. Remove the chicken from their bags and pile on to the noodles, reserving the cooking juices. Strain and add to the sauce. Bring it to the boil and add champagne and with a hand blender froth the sauce (if you're feeling particularly creative) and pour over the chicken and garnish with deep fried leeks.

Strawberry risotto with basil ice cream

serves 4

for the strawberry risotto

1/2kg frozen strawberries

1 litre water

200g sugar

200g fresh strawberries diced

200g risotto rice

50g mascarpone

for the basil ice cream

300 ml milk

200 ml double cream

6 egg yolks

125g sugar

16 basil leaves

To make the ice cream, beat the yolks and sugar together. Slowly bring the milk and cream to the boil and stir into the egg mixture and return to the heat until the mixture reaches 80°C. Put the basil leaves in the bottom of a fine sieve and pass the liquid through them to allow the basil flavours to infuse with the mixture. Repeat this process again, making sure all the egg threads are removed. Leave to cool before churning in an ice-cream maker or alternatively, freeze in a carton and hand stir a few times while it freezes to avoid crystals forming.

For the risotto, cover the frozen strawberries in a pan with 1litre of water and 200g sugar and cook for about 15 minutes and then sieve. Rinse the risotto rice and heat in a pan with a little butter, adding enough of the strawberry stock to cover and cook. Keep adding enough stock until the rice is cooked, which should take about 10-15 minutes.

Finally to make strawberry tuilles, slice the fresh strawberries 4mm thick and on a baking tray, arrange into circles and brush with the stock syrup and dry in the oven at 100°C/Gas Mark 1/2 until crisp.

Similarly take 4 basil leaves and blanche in boiling water, refresh in cold water and then place on the baking tray and brush with olive oil and more of the stock syrup. Dust with icing sugar and dry in the oven also at 100°C/Gas Mark 1/2.

To serve, fold the mascarpone into the diced strawberries and divide into bowls. Put a dried strawberry disc on the top followed by quenelles of ice cream and garnish with a dried basil leaf.

THE QUEENSBERRY

Jason Horn

Open ravioli of langoustine and ceps with grain mustard butter sauce

serves 4

12 large langoustines

200g large fresh ceps, bases trimmed and thickly sliced

2 tablespoons olive oil

30g butter

2 teaspoons chervil

for the ravioli pasta

225g '00' pasta flour or plain flour

2 medium eggs and 2 yolks - beaten

1 teaspoon olive oil

salt and freshly ground white pepper

for the grain mustard butter sauce

50g diced shallot

2 tablespoons white wine vinegar

4 tablespoons dry white wine

6 tablespoons fish stock

2 tablespoons double cream

175g unsalted butter

To make the pasta, place all the ingredients together in a mixer with a dough hook or a food processor and blend until it forms a dough. Tip out onto a work surface and kneed for about 4-5 minutes until smooth and elastic. Wrap in cling film and leave to rest for 1 hour. If you have a pasta machine, roll the pasta through 3 times but set to the finest setting for the final time. Otherwise, use a rolling pin, this may not be as easy but it will do the job. Cut the pasta into 3" squares. Bring a saucepan of salted water to the boil and add a drop of olive oil, add the pasta and cook for 1 minute. Drain and allow to cool. Place the pasta on an oiled tray to prevent them sticking together.

For the mustard butter sauce, place the shallots, white wine vinegar and the fish stock in a pan and simmer until nearly all the liquid has evaporated. Add the double cream and reduce a little more. Remove from the heat and whisk in the butter a little at a time until it has amalgamated. Strain through a sieve, add the mustard and check seasoning. Keep in a warm place.

Bring another large pan of salted water to the boil and drop in the langoustines. Boil for 1 minute, drain and cool. When you are able to handle them, (they are slightly easier to peel when warm), remove the heads, then crack the top of the shell and peel. (Put the shell to the side, this can be used to infuse the fish stock).

To cook the ceps, heat a frying pan, add 1 tablespoon of olive oil and 30g butter. When melted add the ceps and cook for 2 minutes. Season then remove from the pan, add the langoustines, cook for 1-2 minutes, season and add the ceps again, check the seasoning, remove from the pan and keep warm.

Place the pre-cooked pasta squares into some boiling salted water just to heat up again, then remove drain and slightly dry the sheets.

To serve, place one sheet onto a warm plate, add a couple of langoustines and a few ceps on top, place another sheet and repeat. Finally, place a sheet on the top but do not cover. Pour the warm sauce around the side, add the chopped chervil and serve.

Roast saddle of venison, Tuscany cabbage with spiced poached pear

serves 4

4 x 175g venison noisettes

2 tablespoons olive oil

4 tablespoons of port

1 teaspoon of crushed juniper berries

150ml of game or chicken stock

salt and pepper

60g diced unsalted butter - kept cold

for the marinade

$^1/_2$ bottle red wine

$^1/_4$ bottle port

5 white peppercorns

5 juniper berries

2 bay leaves

2 sprigs of thyme

2 shallots, sliced

Warm all the ingredients together, then allow to cool. Marinate the venison for 4-6 hours.

for the poached pear

4 small conference or rocha pears, peeled

juice of half a lemon

1 litre of white wine

250ml cider vinegar

250ml white wine vinegar

400g sugar

2 star anise and 4 cloves

1 teaspoon coriander seeds

1 teaspoon cardamom pods

1 small red chilli, cut in half

$^1/_2$ cinnamon stick

zest of 1 orange

for the cabbage

500g Tuscany cabbage, sliced

50g diced pancetta

50g diced onion

20g unsalted butter

salt and pepper

To cook the venison, brush off the marinade and dry the meat on kitchen paper. Heat the olive oil in a frying pan, add the seasoned venison and cook for about 4-5 minutes on each side, set aside and keep warm. Add the port, crushed juniper berries and 4 tablespoons of the pear liquid (see below) and reduce by half, then add the stock and reduce again by half, strain into a clean pan. Slowly add the diced butter and whisk until it has amalgamated, check seasoning.

Bring all the ingredients (less the pears) for the pear recipe to the boil in a large pan. Reduce heat and add the whole pears. Place a lid or a plate on top to keep them under the liquid and simmer for 20-25 minutes. When cooked remove from the liquid and set aside.

To cook the cabbage, heat a large pan, add the butter and pancetta, cook for 3-4 minutes until the onions and pancetta start to colour. Add the cabbage then turn down the heat, stir, place a lid on top and cook for 5 minutes, season and set aside.

To serve, place the cabbage in the middle of the plate, slice the venison and arrange on the cabbage. Fan the pear and place on the top of the venison, drizzle the sauce around the plate.

Banana and praline soufflé

serves 4

85g toasted hazelnuts

85g caster sugar

4 tablespoons water

for the caramel sauce

62g caster sugar

125ml double cream

Gently heat the sugar until amber in colour. Warm the cream and gently pour into the caramel.

for the soufflé

8 egg whites

110g caster sugar

310ml pastry cream

395ml milk

1 vanilla pod

6 egg yolks

55g flour

2-3 bananas

To make the pastry cream, bring the milk and vanilla pod to the boil. Whisk egg yolks and sugar together, then add the flour and pour onto the milk. Pass through a sieve into a pan and whisk up to the boil.

To make the praline, heat the sugar and water until dissolved and amber in colour. Add the hazelnuts and pour onto a greased baking sheet and leave to cool. When cool blitz in a blender until coarse. Use this to line the ramekins, which have been double buttered with soft butter.

To make the soufflé, take the pastry cream and as an option add hazelnut/banana liqueur. Whisk egg whites into stiff peaks and gradually add the sugar. Mix $1/3$ of the egg white into the pastry cream, then gently fold in the rest of the egg white mixture. Half fill the ramekins, add a layer of sliced banana, then top with remaining soufflé, tap gently and smooth level across the top with a palette knife and run your finger around the rim of the ramekin to ensure a neat finish. Cook for 10-12 minutes 190°C/Gas Mark 5 and serve immediately.

CITY CAFE

BIRMINGHAM

Martin Walker

Minestrone soup with parmesan croûton

serves 8

The tomato broth which is the base for this version takes about 3 hours to cook, but is well worth the wait.

for the broth

3kg ripe tomatoes, plum are the best

150g carrots, chopped

150g celery, chopped

150g shallots, chopped

125g tomato purée

1 star anise

8 coriander seeds

10 white peppercorns

1 bayleaf

1 cardamom pod

4 cloves garlic

1 bunch thyme/basil

for the bacon pellets garnish

2 rashers of bacon

I clove garlic

20g chopped parsley

for the brunoise (finely diced mixed vegetables)

2 carrots, chopped

2 shallots, chopped

3 celery sticks, chopped

1 courgette, chopped

1 leek, chopped

for the parmesan croûton

1 baguette

olive oil

25g grated parmesan

To make the broth, roast the tomatoes for 30 minutes. Meanwhile sweat off all the vegetables and spices until soft, added tomato purée and cook for 5 further minutes. Add the roasted tomatoes to the pot, cover with water and bring to the boil and simmer for 1¹/2 hours, skimming regularly. Remove from the heat and leave to stand for 30 minutes, then strain.

For the bacon pellets, blend together and roll into small balls.

For each parmesan croûton, take a ¹/2" slice of the baguette, brush both sides with olive oil, then bake in the oven for 10 minutes at 180°C/Gas Mark 4. Remove from oven, sprinkle with grated parmesan, then replace in the oven for a further 5 minutes or until golden brown.

To serve, put a dash of olive oil in a pan and saute all the brunoise ingredients and the bacon pellets for 2 minutes. Add to the broth and gently simmer for 10 minutes. Add freshly picked herbs and serve with a Parmesan croûton.

Braised bavette of beef

serves 4

6 bavettes/flanks of beef

400g mirepoix

1 bayleaf

1 sprig thyme

1 sprig rosemary

750ml red wine

salt

pepper

2 litres good chicken stock

1 litre good veal stock

4 carrots, roasted whole

for the mash

1 kg mashed potatoes

$^1/_2$ honey roast parsnip

50g butter

seasoning

for the parsnip crisps

1 parsnip, thinly sliced and deep fried

Season and seal the beef in a hot pan and place in casserole dish. Caramelise the mirepoix vegetables ie celery stick, leek, onion and carrot in the same pan and add to the casserole with the herbs. Pour on the wine and stocks, season and bring to the boil. Place the lid on the casserole and cook for 2 hours at Gas Mark 4 until tender.

When cooked, remove the meat and reduce the cooking liquor to a sauce consistency and strain into a clean pot.

For the mash, mix together all the ingredients and season.

To serve, slice the roasted carrots diagonally and arrange in the centre of each plate. Place a generous amount of mash on the top and place one bavette of beef on top of the mash. Pour the sauce over the beef and garnish with a few parsnip crisps.

Pear and almond tatin

Serves 6

6 large pears

100g whole blanched almonds

200g caster sugar

100g unsalted butter

*6 puff pastry discs
(slightly bigger than the pan)*

200g pistachio nuts, crushed

6 balls cardamom ice cream

Peel, core and slice the pears. To make the caramel, heat the butter and sugar together until it thickens and becomes dark brown in appearance. Pour into 6 blini pans. Place the pears neatly in the pan with some of the almonds and cook on a gentle heat for 10 minutes. Place the pastry disc on top and cook in the oven at 200°C/Gas Mark 6 for a further 15 minutes or until the pastry has cooked.

To serve, turn out onto plates and drizzle excess caramel around the plate. Place 1 ball of cardamom ice cream on top and sprinkle with crushed pistachio.

FAIRYHILL

Adrian Coulthard

Dill and chilli cured salmon with cucumber and crème fraîche

serves 4

1 kg salmon, ideally a tailpiece
(preferably organic)

*Ask the fishmonger to fillet,
skin and pin bone the salmon.*

1 cucumber

1 x 200g tub crème fraîche

for the cure

1 bunch of dill chopped

1/2 bunch of chives chopped

3 tablespoons Demerara sugar

1 1/2 tablespoons coarse sea salt

1/2 tablespoon coarse ground black pepper

zest of 1 lime

1/2 finely chopped green chilli

Combine the cure ingredients (save a little dill for the garnish) and place two thirds between the two fillets, place in a dish or tray and scatter over the remaining third. Cover with cling film and refrigerate overnight, in the morning pour off the resulting liquid and turn the fish over. Refrigerate again and leave for another day. Remove from the fridge and wash away most of the coating, pat dry and wrap in cling film. The fish is now ready to use and will keep for up to 4 days.

Firstly, peel and de-seed the cucumber, then cut the flesh into a _ centimetre dice. Place this in a sieve and sprinkle with salt, weigh down gently if possible and put the sieve over a bowl to drain, leave for at least 1 hour.

Using a very sharp knife, cut the cucumber skin into very thin matchsticks, these need to be about 4 or 5cms long, you will need about 36. Place them in a bowl of iced water to make them curl.

Cut the salmon into the same size dice as the cucumber. Wash the cucumber flesh under running water and dry thoroughly. In a bowl whip the crème fraîche until stiff.

To serve, add the cucumber flesh and salmon to the crème fraîche, taste and season if required. In the middle of each plate, place a ring and fill with the mixture, remove the ring and place cucumber curls around. If desired drizzle a little citrus based vinaigrette into the curls just before serving.

For a taste of real luxury garnish with a little caviar!

The cucumber curls can be omitted if desired although they are worth the work for the presentation.

Suprême of free-range chicken with a vegetable and pearl barley broth

serves 4

2 free-range chickens

a selection of vegetables, ideally:

swede

carrot

celery

courgette

pak choi or greens

40g pearl barley

homemade chicken stock

one glass white wine

The basis of this dish is a good stock. It is worth making this yourself but many supermarkets now have adequate fresh stocks that are not too salty.

To make this dish you will need one chicken breast per person, so in an ideal world buy 1 fresh free-range chicken for every 2 people, remove the breasts and legs and use the carcass for the stock. The legs could be used for another meal later in the week or frozen for another day.

Check your barley, it may need to be soaked before cooking. Cook it, drain and cool under running water, put to one side.

In a large pan brown off the carcass, a mixture of root vegetables or trimmings and an onion. When they have browned, but not burnt, add water, a bay leaf and a few peppercorns. Bring to the boil and turn down to a low simmer, after 2 hours, pour the liquid into another pan and discard the solids.

You should have a good clear stock that is lightly flavoured. Reduce to about 1 litre and add the vegetables and pre-cooked barley.

The choice of vegetables is entirely to your own taste but as you can see from the picture a good mix of colour is essential.

In total you want approximately 100/150 grams per person. Cut the vegetables into pieces that are roughly the same size, add the vegetables to the stock starting with those that take the longest to cook. Swede and carrot first, then celery and courgette followed by the pak choi at the last minute.

Meanwhile cook the chicken; ideally start it off in a frying pan with the minimum amount of oil and then transfer to the oven 190°C/Gas Mark 5 for about 20 minutes to cook through.

When all the vegetables are almost cooked, add the cooked barley, a little white wine, and adjust the seasoning.

To serve, transfer the vegetables with a slotted spoon to the serving dishes and place the chicken on top. Check seasoning and consistency of the stock again and pour around.

Apple and tarragon tart

serves 4

4kg cooking apples

4 Granny Smith apples

a bunch tarragon

12 sheets filo pastry

melted butter

icing sugar

crème fraîche

lemon juice

Take the cooking apples, peel and core, make an apple purée either with a little water in a saucepan over a gentle heat or in a jug in the microwave, add a few drops of lemon juice and work as quickly as possible so that the purée doesn't colour. Put to one side to cool.

Take 6 sheets of pastry and build up the layers, buttering between each sheet and sprinkling with icing sugar. Cut the sheet down the middle and then using a suitable sized cutter or guide, fold or roll the edges up to form the crusts of 2 tart cases and repeat. Place the 4 cases on a baking sheet and bake for 5 minutes at 200°C/Gas Mark 6. Remove from the oven and gently lift off the sheet to allow the bottoms to dry out a little.

Meanwhile chop a couple of sprigs of the tarragon and add to the apple purée and sweeten to taste. Peel the eating apples, core and slice thinly then place in water and lemon juice.

Fill the cases with the apple purée, top with the finely sliced apple, brush with melted butter and sprinkle with icing sugar. Place in the oven and bake for 10-15 minutes or until golden brown. Serve immediately, garnishing with a sprig of fresh tarragon and crème fraîche.

THE MARCLIFFE AT PITFODELS

Michael Stoddart

Ravioli of langoustines, shellfish velouté

serves 4

24 langoustines
2 chopped shallots
1 egg white
4 basil leaves
salt and pepper

for the pasta

250g "OO" flour
2 whole eggs
2 large egg yolks
1 tablespoon olive oil
1 tablespoon water
2 pinches saffron

for the shellfish velouté

langoustine shells
25g shallots
25g carrot
25g leek, white part only
25g celery
150g butter
200ml cognac
1.14 litres chicken stock
290ml double cream
25g cold butter
2 plum tomatoes
2 bay leaves

250 g spinach leaves
2g butter
fresh grated nutmeg
salt and pepper

To make the pasta, infuse the saffron into warmed water and leave to cool. Add all the ingredients together and beat on a medium speed until a dough is formed. Wrap in cling film and refrigerate.

Remove the tails from the langoustine heads and keep for the sauce. Peel the tails and remove the intestine. Place half the tails in a processor with the finely chopped shallots, egg white, salt and pepper and blend to a purée.

In a thick-bottomed pan, add the butter and vegetables that have been finely chopped and sweat them for 5 minutes. Add the langoustine shells and heads and plum tomatoes, cook for a further 10 minutes. Deglaze with cognac and flambé. Add the chicken stock, bring to the boil, add bay leaves and simmer for 30 minutes. Pass the liquor through a fine strainer (muslin if possible) and reduce the stock by half, add the double cream and simmer until it coats the back of a spoon. Finish by whisking in the butter and keep warm.

Pass the pasta dough through the finest setting of a pasta machine and cut out 8, 70mm discs. Share out equal amounts of the langoustine filling and place a basil leaf on top of each. Water the edges of the ravioli and top with a lid. Pinch together and trim with the cutter.

Place the ravioli in boiling water for 5-6 minutes. In a saucepan, with a splash of olive oil, sear the remaining langoustines, season and set aside on a warm place. In the same pan add the butter and wilt the spinach leaves.

To serve, take 4 hot plates and place the spinach in the centre with the 3 tails on top and finish with a piece of ravioli. Reheat the velouté and drizzle over the ravioli and around the plate, garnish with chervil and serve.

Roast breast of pheasant, confit leg, sauté cêpes, morel and thyme jus

serves 4

2 pheasants

1/2 caul fat
(available from butcher)

170g butter

4 Savoy cabbage leaves

6 cêpes sliced

55g dried morels sautéed in water

thyme leaves

4 large potatoes

for the confit

1.14 litres of goose fat or duck fat

1 orange-juice and zest

6 juniper berries crushed

1 sprig of thyme

1 sprig of rosemary

2 cloves of confit garlic

2g Maldon sea salt

2 bay leaves

2 star anise

for the sauce

1.14 litres of game stock

200 ml port wine

pheasant trimming

2 tablespoons olive oil

1 teaspoon cold butter

salt and pepper

the following for the mirepoix

carrot

leek

shallots

celery

for the fondant potato and turnip

1 large potato

1 small peeled turnip

290ml chicken stock

1 teaspoon chopped thyme leaves

110g butter

black pepper and sea salt to taste

First remove the legs from the pheasant and remove the feet (your butcher will do this for you). Remove the underside of the carcass and cut into small pieces. Put aside the legs and crowns of the pheasant. To confit the legs first as they take the longest, season with the salt, orange juice, zest and star anise and place in a heavy pan skin-side down and pour in the goose fat or duck fat. Put the confit on to boil, skim and leave to cook slowly for 1 1/2 hours. When ready, remove the legs and flake all the meat from the bones.

Place the cabbage leaves into boiling water and blanch them, refresh in iced water and pat dry. Lay out a cabbage leaf, season and place a quarter of the leg meat into the centre. Using a cloth, shape the cabbage into a ball. Repeat and wrap them in a piece of caul fat. Refrigerate

For the sauce, take the pheasant trimmings and mirepoix and brown them in the olive oil. Deglaze with the port and reduce until it is syrupy, add the game stock and bring to the boil. Skim and simmer until reduced to 570ml, pass through a muslin cloth and keep warm.

Slice the potato tops off lengthways and punch out 4 x 60mm discs of potato. Cut the turnip into 1" thick slices and punch 4 discs from them. Take a shallow non-stick pan; add 4g of softened butter, the potatoes, and turnip followed by the chicken stock, thyme, salt and pepper. Heat the pan and brown both sides of the discs. Put the pan in the oven 180°C/Gas Mark 4 for about 30 minutes and keep moving the fondants around so they don't stick.

Brown the pheasant on the skin-

side, season and place in the oven with the fondants. In a little butter, seal all the cabbage and confit parcels and place into the oven to heat.

To serve, take 4 warm plates, place the fondants at the top, confit parcel on the turnip and remove the breasts from the crowns. Sauté the cêpes and morels, scatter around the plate. Place a breast of pheasant on the front and pour the pheasant jus around and serve.

Roast breast of pheasant, confit leg, sauté cêpes, morel and thyme jus

Dark chocolate and raspberry tart with mascarpone ice cream

Dark chocolate and raspberry tart with mascarpone ice cream

serves 4

9g butter

170g caster sugar

4 vanilla pods

2 eggs

500g flour

for the chocolate filling

400g dark chocolate finely chopped

150ml milk

210ml double cream

2 eggs

1^1/$_2$ punnets fresh raspberries

1 punnet for garnish

for the mascarpone ice cream

250g mascarpone

4 egg yolks

70g icing sugar

1 teaspoon vanilla extract

Place the butter and sugar in a mixing machine and beat until soft, add the eggs and beat in the scraped vanilla seeds. Add the flour and mix. Remove the dough, wrap in cling film and refrigerate.

Place the chopped chocolate in a bowl and cover with the boiled milk and cream, whisk in the eggs and set to one side.

For the ice cream, whisk the icing sugar and egg yolks together until white, add the vanilla extract and fold in the mascarpone cheese. Place into a sterilised container and freeze.

Line an 8" flan ring with the vanilla pastry and let the pastry overlap the edge. Blind bake the pastry until light golden with baking beans at 180°C/Gas Mark 4. Remove the flan and bake for a further 4 minutes without

the beans. Arrange the raspberries inside the flan case standing up, then pour in the chocolate custard. Tap the tray and remove any air bubbles with a small knife.

Bake the tart at 130°/Gas Mark 1^1/$_2$ until it has set, let it cool and refrigerate. To remove the tart take a small knife and trim the overlapping pastry, remove the ring and you should have a neat edge round the chocolate tart.

To serve, cut into 8 portions with a very hot knife, liberally dust the individual tarts with icing sugar and blow torch them to form a caramelised crust. Place the tart on a plate. Arrange 5 raspberries in a small ring and top with a ball of mascarpone ice cream.

THE SWAN HOTEL

Shaun Naen

Colston Bassett Stilton brûlée with red onion and black olive biscottini

serves 4

150g Colston Bassett Stilton, grated

570ml double cream

2 whole eggs

2 egg yolks

^{1}/2teaspoon flaky sea salt

1 tablespoon chopped chives

a pinch of grated nutmeg

^{1}/2 teaspoon ground white pepper

for the black olive biscottini

50g pine kernels

100g olive paste

250g plain flour

1 teaspoon baking powder

^{1}/2 teaspoon black pepper

1 teaspoon fennel seeds

100g grated Parmesan cheese

3 whole eggs, beaten

for the caramelised red onion

1 large red onion

4 tablespoons of olive oil

50ml sherry vinegar

100g Demerara sugar

salt and pepper

To make the brûlée, bring the cream to the boil in a saucepan and then add the grated cheese and stir in well with a wooden spoon until the cheese has melted. Beat the whole eggs, yolks and sea salt until pale and fluffy. Pour the cream mixture into the egg mixture and whisk it vigorously until both mixtures are well mixed together. Sprinkle in the nutmeg, pepper and chives. Skim the top of the mixture and pour into an ovenproof dish or ramekin moulds. Place in a roasting tin, fill with water half way up the dishes and put in a preheated oven 100°C/Gas Mark ^{1}/2 and cook for about 30-45 minutes. Remove it from the oven and leave to cool. Chill in the fridge to set, until the dish is ready to be served.

For the biscottini, put all the ingredients in a clean mixing bowl and blend them together until the mixture forms into a smooth dough. Take it out of the bowl and knead it on a work surface for a minute. Wrap it up in cling film and chill in the fridge for 30 minutes to rest. Cut the dough into 4 and roll to form 'French baguette' shapes. Place them onto a baking tray lined with greaseproof paper and egg wash the tops. Bake in a pre-heated oven, 180°C/Gas Mark 4 for 30 minutes or until they sound hollow when tapped. Take the bread out of the oven and leave them to cool for a few minutes, then slice them at an angle and return to the oven for 5-10 minutes until they become crispy.

To make the caramelised red onion, peel and slice the onion. Heat the olive oil in a frying pan and sauté the onion gently, but do not let the onion discolour. Add the sherry vinegar and leave it to simmer until it has evaporated. Then put in the Demerara sugar and keep stirring until it caramelises, season with salt and pepper to taste.

Braised lamb noisette with five-spice scented sauce

serves 4

1 noisette of lamb,
short cut, oven-ready

1 carrot, peeled and diced

1/2 celery stick, peeled and diced

1/2 leek, washed and diced

4-5 shallots, chopped

1 garlic clove, chopped

1 teaspoon Chinese five-spice

1 cinnamon stick

50ml olive oil

500ml red wine

500ml chicken stock

for the garnish

100g broad beans,
peeled and blanched

100g haricot beans,
soaked and simmered until cooked

1 large red pepper, skinned and
roasted and cut into 2mm squares

100g lamb sweetbread,
blanched and skinned

Ask the butcher to trim and tie the lamb noisette like a sausage. Season with salt and pepper and seal in a little olive oil in a frying pan until golden brown. Transfer the meat to an ovenproof pot and leave it to one side. Pour the excess oil from the pan, return to the heat and sauté the carrot, celery, leek, shallots, garlic and five-spice. Caramelise the ingredients until the flavour comes through, add the red wine and simmer until the wine reduces to half of the original amount and then add the chicken stock and cinnamon stick. Bring the liquid to the boil and pour it into the ovenproof pot containing the lamb; the meat should be well covered.

Place the pot in a preheated oven 100°C/Gas Mark 1/2 and cook for 20-30 minutes or until the meat is just pink in colour. Remove the meat from the pot and strain the liquid into a clean saucepan. Return to the stove, skim the top and slowly reduce the sauce until it coats the back of the spoon. Season to taste.

For the garnish, slice the sweetbread into 3 pieces and dust with plain flour. Heat the frying pan with 2 tablespoons of olive oil. Fry the sweetbread pieces until golden brown, remove and place onto kitchen paper to soak up the excess oil. For the beans and red pepper, sauté in a saucepan with a knob of butter and seasoning.

To serve, trim off both ends of the lamb and cut into 4 pieces, place about 3 tablespoons of the beans and diced red peppers in the centre of each plate and put a piece of the lamb noisette on top. Lastly place the sweetbreads on top of the lamb and then spoon the sauce around the plate. Finish it off with a sprinkle of flaky sea salt.

Three peppered iced parfait with caramelised peppered pineapple

erves 4

1 medium size pineapple

480g caster sugar

300ml water

100ml white wine

1 cinnamon stick

1 tablespoon pink peppercorns

1 tablespoon black peppercorns, roughly crushed

1 tablespoon Sichuan peppers

1 dried red chilli

1 orange, peeled and juiced

1 lemon, peeled and juiced

for the three peppered iced parfait

1 tablespoon pink peppercorns

1 tablespoon black peppercorns, roughly crushed

1 tablespoon Sichuan peppers

225g caster sugar

100ml water

6 egg yolks

25g caster sugar

1 teaspoon vanilla extract

600ml double cream, lightly whipped

To make the caramelised peppered pineapple, start by making the syrup. In a deep saucepan, put all the ingredients together, (except the pineapple) and give it a good whisk. Place the saucepan on a medium heat and bring to the boil for about 1 minute. Peel the pineapple, cut out the eyes and slice it into 4 equal sizes. Place the sliced pineapple in an ovenproof dish and pour all the syrup in until it covers the pineapple slices. Cover with a lid and place the dish in a preheated oven on 120°C/Gas Mark 1¹/2 and cook for about 3 hours. Remove the pineapple slices from the dish and strain the syrup into a clean deep saucepan, return to the stove and reduce the syrup until soft crack stage on your thermometer. Put the pineapple back into the syrup and leave until ready to serve.

For the three-peppered iced parfait, put the 3 peppers, sugar and water in a sugar pan and give it a good whisk. Take a pastry brush dipped in cold water and brush off the excess sugar inside the side of the pan. Place the pan on a medium heat and slowly bring to the boil with a thermometer inside. Keep brushing the inside of the pan to prevent crystallisation. Meanwhile, whisk the egg yolk, sugar and vanilla extract in a mixing bowl until pale and fluffy. Continue to boil the syrup until it reaches a temperature of 120°C then take the syrup off the heat and plunge it into cold water for a few seconds. Slowly trickle the syrup into the egg mixture and carry on whisking on full speed until it is double the volume and fluffy. In another clean bowl, lightly whip the cream. Whisk in one quarter of the cream into the egg mixture, then slowly fold in the rest of the cream keeping the mixture light. Prepare a 5 x 5 mm ring, tightly cover one end with cling film and pour the parfait mixture into the ring and freeze until firm.

NUTHURST GRANGE COUNTRY HOUSE

Ben Davies

Assiette of goat's cheese

serves 4

¹/₂ goat's cheese log

2 Crottin of goat's cheese

2 sheets of feuille de bric pastry (available from a good delicatessen)

2 sun-dried tomatoes, chopped

3 basil leaves, chopped

1 potato, grated and made into galettes (flat, round cakes)

50g wild mushrooms, washed and cooked

1 apple, peeled and diced

25g walnuts

2 slices brioche

a handful of salad leaves

Balsamic vinegar

Thai green curry dressing

olive oil

Dice the goat's cheese log and add the basil and sun-dried tomatoes. Wrap in the bric pastry like a spring roll. Dice the other half and marinate in a little olive oil and herbs. Cut the two Crottins in half and rub with olive oil, salt and pepper, then toast the brioche. Mix the mushrooms with the Balsamic vinegar and a little olive oil. Cook the spring rolls in a deep fat fryer until golden brown.

To serve, arrange the different cheeses on the plate using a salad garnish with half a parcel, the brioche and Crottin, a little diced apple and walnuts, the millefeuille and dress with the various vinaigrettes.

Char grilled loin of lamb and cutlet, served with a tarte tatin of vegetables and a thyme and tomato sauce

serves 4

2 x 7 bone best end of lamb
(French trimmed)

110g puff pastry

2 large potatoes

4 each of baby leeks, baby carrots,
baby turnips, baby artichokes,
caramelised shallots, sun-dried
tomatoes and basil leaves

290ml lamb stock

freshly picked thyme

3 tomatoes, skinned,
de-seeded and diced

55g butter

Cut one and a half of the loins of lamb down to the eye of the meat. Trim the remaining half of the loin to the cutlets, removing all the fat and skin.

Roll out the puff pastry thinly and prick it with a fork, then cut into discs about 1cm larger than the pan you are going to make the tarte tatin in. (We use small blinis frying pans). Line the pans with a little olive oil, salt and pepper and then arrange the peeled and blanched baby vegetables with the herbs, shallots and sun-dried tomatoes. Season again and cover with the pastry.

Cook the loins and cutlets of lamb on a char grill or a griddle pan until nicely marked and finish in the oven. Place the tarte tatins in an oven at 180°C/Gas Mark 5 for approximately 15 minutes or until crisp and golden brown. Peel the potatoes and ball with a parissiene scoop and sauté in a little oil and butter until golden brown.

To serve, turn the tarts out and arrange on the plates. Heat the sauce with the thyme, add the tomato and pour around the lamb and potatoes.

Dark chocolate soufflé

serves 8

A nice rich way to finish the meal, after two reasonably healthy courses

$^1/_2$ litre of water

150g cocoa powder

10 egg whites

300g caster sugar

Boil the water, whisk on the cocoa powder and remove from the heat. Pass the mixture through a sieve. Line 8 ramekin moulds with butter and sugar. Place the 10 egg whites in a clean mixing bowl. Mix the whites to a soft peak, add the sugar and then whisk to a stiff peak. Gently fold into the chocolate mixture taking care not to deflate the egg white. Pour into each of the ramekins and level off with the back of a knife. With your thumb, remove any excess mixture from the inside of the ramekin. Place in a pre-heated oven at 200°C/Gas Mark 6 for five minutes.

To serve, remove from the oven, and sprinkle with icing sugar.

MORSTON HALL HOTEL & RESTAURANT

Galton Blackiston

Twice baked cheese soufflé

serves 8-10

425ml milk

slice of onion

pinch of nutmeg

75g butter

75g plain flour

pinch of dry English mustard

250g grated strong cheddar cheese

6 eggs, separated

salt and pepper

425ml cream

Butter the inside of 10 ramekins. Heat the milk with the slice of onion and nutmeg. Bring to the boil and remove the onion. In a separate pan, melt the butter, stir in the flour and mustard powder and bind together. Now slowly add the milk and stir constantly until smooth.

Remove from the heat and add the grated cheddar and stir in the egg yolks and season. Whisk the egg whites until stiff, fold into the cheese mixture and fill the ramekins. Wipe a clean finger around the inside rim for a neat finish. Cover the bottom of a roasting pan with boiling water for the ramekins to stand in and bake the soufflés at 190°C/Gas Mark 5 for approximately 20 minutes.

Remove from the oven and allow to sink and cool. Turn them out onto a buttered baking tray. Turn the oven up to 200°C/Gas Mark 7. Sprinkle soufflés with extra cheddar and coat with the cream and bake again for approximately 15 minutes.

Serve on a salad of ripe peeled and sliced tomatoes, liberally sprinkled with chives and a good spoonful of the rich cheese sauce.

Warm mousse of chicken and Roquefort

serves 8

350g chicken breast,
skin removed and diced

1 egg white

425ml double cream

pepper

110g Roquefort cheese
or Stilton or Lanark Blue

This recipe can be made in the morning and steamed later in the evening.

Place the chicken breast into a liquidiser and purée well. Scrape around the outsides and blitz again, adding the egg white. Once well puréed, take out of the machine and push the raw mixture through not too fine a sieve or it will take too long. Place the purée into a large bowl and slowly pour in the cream, stir with a spatula until the cream is incorporated and the mixture is of dropping consistency. Then fold in thumb nail size pieces of the Roquefort cheese. Season with pepper only.

Now using perforated cling film about 10 inches square, place a good dollop of chicken mousse into the middle, bring the 4 corners together, wrap up tightly tying a knot in the end and make into a tight ball. Refrigerate until the evening, then place the balls into a steamer and gently steam for about 20 minutes until 'wobbly'. Take out and using scissors, cut the cling film to release the ball of mousse.

Serve with a tomato butter sauce and sautéed spinach.

Baked Alaska

Baked Alaska

serves 6-8

6 eggs separated

175g plain flour

160g caster sugar

$^1/_2$ pot of strawberry jam

$^1/_2$ tub of vanilla ice cream

for the Italian meringue

110g egg whites

225g caster sugar

55ml water

Line a 10 x 12" (25cm) tray with greaseproof paper.

Place the egg whites into a mixing bowl, whisk until stiff and gradually add the sugar. Once it is all whisked in, add one egg yolk at a time and combine, then fold in the flour. Place the mixture into your prepared tray and spread evenly. Bake at 220°C/Gas Mark 6 for 10 minutes until springy to touch. Once the sponge has cooled, cut out 3 half-inch rings and place on a baking tray with a dessertspoon full of jam in the middle.

For the meringue, place the sugar and water into a thick-bottomed pan over a medium heat. Using a sugar thermometer, take the sugar and water mixture to 115°C (soft ball stage) this is achieved by leaving it to boil for about 3-4 minutes. When the sugar is almost at 110°C turn on your machine and start to whisk your egg whites, then pour over the sugar mixture very slowly-- little by little. Be very careful this sugar mixture is extremely hot.

Once all combined, the mixture will increase in size. Leave the machine on mixing until cool for about 3 minutes. Once cooled place into a piping bag with a star nozzle.

Place a ball of vanilla ice cream onto the jam in the middle of the sponge, then cover with meringue from the sponge base to the tip of the ice cream. Make sure all the ice cream is covered with meringue and sealed in.

Bake at 210°C/Gas Mark 6/7 for 3-4 minutes until golden brown on top. Serve immediately with crème a l'Anglaise or pouring cream.

ETTINGTON PARK HOTEL

Sonia Fitzsimons

Cornish crab and smoked sea trout with dill, marinated cucumber and horseradish cream

serves 4

200g Cornish crab meat

125g smoked sea trout

1/2 cucumber, finely diced

1 teaspoon fresh dill, chopped

1 tablespoon white wine vinegar

1 tablespoon caster sugar

50g caviar

1 large bunch of rocket

for the horseradish cream

25g grated horseradish

150g crème fraîche

Peel and dice the cucumber and sprinkle with sea salt. Leave overnight. Rinse well and pat dry. Mix with the dill, vinegar and sugar and season to taste.

Mix the grated horseradish with the crème fraiche and season to taste.

To serve, wash the rocket and place in a circle on the plate. Place a ring mould on top and fill to 1cm with rocket. Mix the crabmeat and cucumber and place a layer in the mould. Next layer the sliced smoked sea trout and finish with a layer of horseradish cream. Spoon the caviar on to the top and remove the mould.

Fillet of red snapper with rice and kidney beans, roast plantain, mango salsa and a coriander and coconut emulsion

serves 4

4 x 200g red snapper fillets

150g rice

100g kidney beans

50g red and yellow pepper, diced

60g red onion, finely diced

1 sprig of thyme

1 sweet potato

1 ripe plantain
(large cooking banana)

250ml chicken stock

for the mango salsa

1/2 mango

1/2 papaya

1 bunch of coriander

1/2 chilli

2 limes

for the coriander and coconut emulsion

200g shallots, diced

butter

1 teaspoon coriander seeds

2 cardamom pods

1 star anise

1 teaspoon Madras curry paste

2 teaspoons turmeric

50ml white wine

500ml fish stock

600ml coconut cream

Soak the red kidney beans overnight, drain and rinse well. Sauté half the finely diced red onion with the diced peppers, add the kidney beans and thyme and cover with the chicken stock. Simmer until the kidney beans are cooked. Add the rice and finish cooking.

For the salsa, mix the rest of the finely diced red onion, mango, papaya and chilli with the limejuice and chopped coriander leaves. Season to taste.

For the emulsion, sweat the shallots with a little butter until soft. Add the spices, curry paste and a bay leaf; and cook for a few minutes. Add the white wine and stock and simmer until dry. Pour in the coconut cream and simmer for 3 minutes to reduce. Season to taste and strain through a fine sieve.

To serve, sauté the snapper fillets skin side first and then finish in the oven. Fry the plantain in oil until golden brown. Roast the sweet potato until soft and caramelised. Place the rice and kidney beans in the middle of the plate and place the snapper on top, then arrange the sweet potato and plantain around it. Quenelle the salsa and place on top of the snapper and drizzle the coriander and coconut emulsion around the plate.

Iced raspberry "trifle" with crème anglaise

serves 4

4 sponge discs

sweet sherry

24 raspberries

for the raspberry sorbet

500g raspberry purée

75ml water

75ml lemon juice

75g caster sugar

2 egg whites,
whisked to soft peaks

for the nougatine parfait

50g caster sugar

22g whole almonds

22g hazelnuts

1 vanilla pod, split

2 large eggs

30g unsalted butter, melted

62g candied fruit, chopped

250ml double cream, whisked to soft peaks

for the lemon verbena ice cream

500ml double cream

12 lemon verbena leaves

4 yolks

125g caster sugar

for the crème anglaise

500ml milk

7 egg yolks

150g caster sugar

1 vanilla pod

Mix all the ingredients for the raspberry sorbet together and churn in a suitable container in the freezer until set.

For the parfait, roast the almonds and hazelnuts until golden, remove the skins and cut up into bite size pieces. Whisk the eggs, sugar and vanilla in a bowl until at the ribbon stage. Gradually add the melted butter and cook over a saucepan on a gentle heat i.e. a bain marie until a figure of 8 is held. When cooled, add the nuts, fruit and fold in the cream.

For the ice cream, bring the double cream to the boil and add the lemon verbena leaves – infuse for 30 minutes. Whisk the sugar and egg yolks together and pour the hot cream over, then whisk together. Return to the stove and cook until the mixture coats the back of a wooden spoon. Remove from the heat and cool quickly. When it is cold, churn until set.

For the crème anglaise, whisk the egg yolks and sugar together. Add the vanilla pod to the milk and bring

to the boil. Pour over the egg mixture and whisk well. Return to the stove and cook until the mixture coats the back of a wooden spoon. Cool quickly.

To serve, soak the sponges in the sherry and place in the bottom of a tall ring mould. Then layer sorbet, parfait and ice cream on the top, allowing each layer to set before adding the next. Garnish with raspberry coulis and crème anglaise.

Richard Lyth

Seared scallops and beetroot, horseradish crème fraîche

serves 4

12 plump fresh scallops (hand-dived if possible), sliced horizontally

24 slices of cooked beetroot, cut to the thickness of a £1 coin

200ml crème fraîche

25g finely grated fresh horseradish (or use horseradish relish to taste)

50ml chilli oil

50ml olive oil

100ml raspberry vinegar

maldon salt

rocket leaves

Combine the vinegar and oils and warm gently. Add the beetroot slices and heat through.

Heat a frying pan, pass the scallops through a little olive oil on a clean plate and place into the pan.

Sear for 30 seconds then flip over and cook a further 15 seconds and season lightly with salt.

To serve, place a spoonful of crème fraîche mixed with the horseradish and lemon juice in the centre of a plate and spread a little. Place the beetroot slices on the cream and top with the scallops. Spoon a little of the beetroot vinaigrette around and decorate with rocket leaves

Smoked haddock on parsley mash with spinach, poached egg and Arran mustard sauce

serves 4

4 x 150g Glasgow pale fillets of smoked haddock

500ml mixed half milk/half water

4 poached eggs

300g leaf spinach, washed

300g mashed potato

50g roughly chopped parsley

150ml white wine, dry

1 finely chopped onion

parsley stalks

150ml whipping cream

50g Arran grain mustard

4 tomatoes, skinned, de-seeded and diced

50g chives into batons

Reduce the wine with the onion and parsley stalks by half. Add the cream and simmer to coating consistency. Strain through a fine sieve. Add the mustard and tomatoes and keep warm. Make your favourite mash and finish with parsley.

Cook the spinach in a little butter in a frying pan, season well with with salt and pepper.

Heat the milk and water together and poach the haddock for 3-4 minutes.

To serve, place the mash in centre of plate. Top with the haddock and spinach and finish with the re- heated poached egg. Spoon over the sauce and sprinkle with chives.

Hot chocolate fondant

serves 4

25g unsalted butter
for greasing moulds

250g unsalted butter

120g egg yolk

250g whole egg

125g caster sugar

50g plain flour

250g broken bitter chocolate
(70% cocoa)

4 balls of ice cream

4 brandy snap biscuits

fruit to garnish

Butter 4 dariole moulds and chill.
Beat the eggs, yolks and sugar until
pale. Put the chocolate and butter
into a bowl and place over a pan of
hot water to melt. Remove from the
heat and gradually add the egg
mixture and beat until smooth. Fold
in the sifted flour and pour into the
chilled moulds and refrigerate
overnight. Bake in a pre heated oven
180°c/Gas Mark 4 for 12-15 minutes.

To serve, carefully remove the
moulds and turn out onto pudding
plates. Finish with your favourite ice
cream and fruit garnish

LONGUEVILLE MANOR

Andrew Baird

Grilled suprême of sea bass with calamari and sauce vierge

serves 4

1.8kg sea bass

225g calamari

450g potato purée

1g ground saffron

14 tablespoons olive oil

110g shallots

2 cups good red wine

2 cups fish stock

$1/2$ cup mixed picked and chopped herbs – basil, parsley, chervil, tarragon, coriander

$1/2$ cup diced tomatoes, skinned and deseeded

1 lemon

2 cloves garlic

Fillet and skin the sea bass and cut into suprêmes, or better still, ask your fishmonger to do this for you.

Warm a little olive oil in a pan and add a clove of crushed garlic. Cook for a few minutes without colouring. Then add the potato purée, saffron and seasoning. Keep warm.

Heat a heavy based frying pan. Add a little oil and let it become quite hot. Place your suprêmes of sea bass in the pan, presented skin side down first. Once the fish has a little colour, place it in a very hot oven to cook for 4 minutes. When ready it should be golden brown and still very moist.

To prepare the sauce vierge, boil and reduce the red wine by half, together with the diced shallots. Add fish stock, boil and reduce by half again. At this point add the diced tomatoes, olive oil and mixed herbs and check seasoning. Do not allow the sauce to get too hot, it only needs to be warm.

To serve, place the saffron potato in the centre of the plate and place the sea bass on top. Carefully spoon around the sauce vierge. Finally, quickly stir-fry the calamari in a very hot pan for about 10 seconds, season and add a squeeze of lemon. Then place on top of the sea bass. Serve with a salad of garden leaves or vegetables of your choice.

Suprême of turbot with tuna rillettes and aromatic herb and noodle salad

serves 4

120g tuna, poached

30g fresh tomato compôte

30g crème fraîche

salt and pepper

lemon juice to taste

baby capers

2 tablespoons olive oil

1 tomato, skinned, deseeded
and chopped

Cabernet Sauvignon dressing
(3 parts oil, 1 part Cabernet
Sauvignon vinegar)

4 x 75g suprêmes of turbot,
skinned and boned

4 deep-fried basil leaves

4 red baby bell peppers

for the chlorophyll noodles

150g chlorophyll (parsley and
watercress) purée

600g 'OO' flour

1 egg

1 teaspoon olive oil

salt

for the noodle salad

20g anchovies

20g sliced red onion

50g sliced red pepper (stewed in
Cabernet Sauvignon vinegar)

10g roasted pine kernels

20g picked herbs; chervil,
coriander and dill

40g French beans,
blanched and sliced

40g tomatoes, skinned, deseeded
and chopped

olive oil

lemon juice

salt and pepper

To make the chlorophyll noodles, blend all the ingredients to form a dough, knead until smooth and rest in the fridge for 1 hour. Using the lowest setting, pass through a pasta machine to make 200g noodles.

Poach the tuna until just cooked through. Remove from poaching liqueur and leave to cool. Once cool, flake with the back of a fork, add tomato compôte and crème fraîche and season with salt, pepper, lemon juice and baby capers and form into a quenelle.

Cook the noodles in separate pans in salted, boiling water with olive oil. Refresh, drain and mix with a little olive oil. Put into a bowl with the remaining ingredients and gently mix. Do not break down the ingredients.

To serve, put the noodle salad into the centre of the plate. Encircle with dressed tomato and Cabernet Sauvignon dressing. Cook turbot in a heavy-based black pan to attain good colouration. Once cooked, place on top of the noodles. Top with the tuna rillettes and finish with deep-fried basil leaf and baby bell pepper.

Summer pudding

serves 4

10 slices of medium white sliced bread
(not too fresh - it can be one day old)

4 cups of mixed garden berries -
strawberries, alpine strawberries,
raspberries, blackberries, tayberries,
local berries, blackcurrants and
redcurrants

1 cup of sugar

2 cups of extra thick Jersey cream

sprigs of mint

for the coulis

3 cups of berries

1 cup of icing sugar

2 cups of berries for garnish

Place the berries for the pudding in a saucepan with the sugar and half a cup of water. Gently bring to simmering point and cook for 2-3 minutes. Drain in a colander and leave to cool keeping the liquid separate.

Cut 8 disks of bread to fit perfectly into the ramekins, 1 for the bottom and 1 for the top, plus 4 strips for around the sides. Soak the bread in the liquid from the summer berries. Line the ramekins, keeping 4 disks aside for the lids. Spoon the berries into ramekins and press down firmly. Top with the last disk and refrigerate, preferably overnight.

To make the coulis, heat the berries in a saucepan and add the icing sugar. Once all the sugar has dissolved (this may happen before it has boiled), liquidise and purée, pass through a fine sieve and leave to cool.

To serve, remove the summer pudding from the ramekin and place on a plate. Pour over the sauce, allowing it to flood. Then carefully arrange the remainder of summer berries around the pudding. Top with whipped Jersey cream and a sprig of mint.

THE HORN OF PLENTY

Peter Gorton

Thai style seafood salad

serves 4

175g cooked mixed seafood
(salmon, prawns, scallops etc)

1 fresh chilli
seeded and cut into fine strips

4 shallots sliced finely

1 tablespoons ginger finely chopped

2 cloves garlic finely chopped

50 ml lime juice

2 tablespoons fish sauce

5 strips sugar

2 tablespoons olive oil

1 iceberg lettuce
or lettuce of your choice

half a cucumber
cut into matchstick size pieces

55g fresh chopped coriander

salt and pepper to taste

Peel and seed the cucumber, cut into matchstick size pieces and add to the cooked seafood. In another bowl add the chillies, shallots, ginger and garlic, toss with the lime juice, fish sauce and the other ingredients. Add to the seafood and cucumber and mix thoroughly, stir in the chopped coriander. Place on top of the crisp iceberg lettuce and garnish with crispy fried potato straws.

Steamed loin of lamb with herbs and a breadcrumb coating

serves 4

24oz best end of lamb, cut into four equal pieces completely boned and trimmed

olive oil

1 tablespoon Dijon mustard (optional)

300g/10oz breadcrumbs

1 bunch fresh parsley

1 tablespoon thyme, chopped

1 tablespoon rosemary, chopped

1 tablespoon basil, chopped

1 teaspoon garlic, chopped

100ml/3 fl oz olive oil plus 2 tablespoons for sealing the lamb

2 large leeks
(outer tough leaves removed)

Wash and blanch the leeks. Heat the oil in a frying pan and seal the lamb fillets on both sides, allow to cool. Blend the breadcrumbs with the herbs, garlic and olive oil. Season with salt and freshly ground pepper and spread a thin layer of mustard over the lamb fillets and coat evenly with the breadcrumbs.

Remove 4 strips of leek lengthways, pat dry and place the lamb fillets on top of the leeks and roll to form a sausage roll shape; make sure the leek completely wraps around the lamb fillets. Place each piece of lamb in cling film and roll up tightly several times to cover. Cook for 10-12 minutes for medium: allow to rest in the cling film for 5 minutes before you carve.

Place a potato dish of your choice into the middle of four pre-heated dinner plates. Cut the lamb into three pieces and arrange around the potato. Serve with a sauce of your choice; red wine or red pepper sauces both go well with lamb.

Crème brûlée with exotic fruit dice

serves 4-6

for the crème brûlée

1pt/16fl oz double cream

5 egg yolks

200g/7oz castor sugar

1 vanilla pod with the seeds scraped out and added to the cream, or 1 tablespoon of vanilla essence

for the exotic fruit dice

cut into small dice:

1 kiwi

1 small mango

1 small papaya

l small fresh pineapple

8oz/225g strawberries cut in half (optional)

Mix fruits together and set aside. Lightly oil the outside of four to six 2³/4" diameter x 1³/4" high rings moulds. Wrap the bottom and lower two thirds of each mould with cling film. Place the moulds upside down on a baking tray in a 150˚C/gas mark 2 for 15 seconds or until the plastic wraps tightly onto the mould. Allow to cool, set aside.

Bring the cream to the boil with the vanilla. Remove from the heat, whisk the sugar and egg yolks together until smooth and white. Slowly pour the hot cream onto the egg yolk mixture and whisk for two minutes or until the mixture starts to thicken. Strain through a fine mesh sieve and pour into the ready prepared moulds. Bake in a water bath at 170˚C/gas 3 or until the custard has set. Drain the water and refrigerate the custard.

Place a 2³/4" ring mould on the centre of one of the plates. Spoon about two tablespoons of the fruit dice into the mould pack tightly and carefully remove the mould. Sprinkle each custard with about 1 tablespoon of sugar and caramelise with a blow torch (or under a hot grill, but do watch carefully) until golden brown. Remove the mould around the custard and gently place on top of the fruit dice. Serve with some raspberry sauce or a sauce of your choice.

WINTERINGHAM FIELDS

Germain Schwab

Cauliflower 'couscous', curry salted tuile and Avruga caviar

serves 6

for the tuile

200g flour

20g sugar

30g salt

8 egg whites

120g melted butter

1 tablespoon mild curry powder

for the cauliflower 'couscous'

3 teaspoons fromage frais

85g (small tin) Avruga caviar

100g cauliflower

oriental spices

Place all the ingredients for the tuile in a liquidiser and blend together. Make a template from a plastic margarine tub lid of about a 2¹/₂ cm diameter circle. Scrape the mixture over the template with a spatula on to a rubber non-stick mat and make a dozen tuile at a time. Bake at 160°C/Gas Mark 2¹/₂ for 7-9 minutes.

For the cauliflower 'couscous', finely grate the cauliflower and place it into a muslin with a little oriental spice, tie into a bag and steam for 4-5 minutes. Open the muslin and allow the cauliflower to cool on a tray before chilling in the fridge. When the cauliflower 'couscous' is totally cold, add a little fromage frais to it. Season with white pepper and salt.

When cool, spread the cauliflower 'couscous' between 2 tuile to form a sandwich, then smooth off the excess mixture from the outside and roll in the Avruga caviar.

Pancake with scallop and Avruga caviar on étuvé of leeks with walnut dressing

serves 6

for the walnut dressing

1 shallot, finely chopped

$^1/_2$ garlic clove, finely chopped

20g walnut pieces

40g tomato, skinned, deseeded and chopped

10g coriander, basil, finely chopped

30ml white wine vinegar

20ml truffle oil

30ml walnut oil

40ml olive oil

salt, pepper and lemon juice

Liquidise all the ingredients together and serve when ready at room temperature.

for the étuvé (stewed) leeks

2 leeks - white part only, sliced coarsely

40g butter

15ml water

salt and pepper

for the pancakes

8 king scallops

40g Avrugar caviar

1 egg

150ml milk

12g salt

30g sugar

1 tablespoon of maple syrup

200g plain flour

3g yeast

2 limes, zest

1 lemon, zest

Heat up a medium sized pan and add the leeks, butter and water to the hot pan and cover with a lid. Cook until tender and season with salt and pepper. Drain.

For the pancakes, zest the lemon and mix into the flour. Add the salt and sugar. Melt the butter, allow to cool then add the egg, milk and yeast. Lightly beat together until smooth. Add maple syrup to the liquid mix and fold into the flour. Allow to prove for 4 hours. To cook, add a knob of butter to 2 non-stick frying pans. Spoon the pancake mixture into the centre of the pans - 2 inches in diameter. Once coloured on the bottom quickly flash the mixture under the grill for approximately 30 seconds. Place the sliced scallops onto the pancakes, overlapping each one. Flip the pancake over onto the scallop side and cook until brown.

To serve, spoon the leeks into a circle approximately 2 inches in diameter onto the centre of the plate. Spoon the dressing around the outside of the leeks. Place both pancakes on top of each other and place on top of the leeks. Place a teaspoon full of Avruga caviar on top of the pancake and serve. Garnish plate with poached scallop livers.

Sauternes jelly with fresh berries

serves 6

1 whole lemon

200g sugar

550ml water

100ml Sauternes

5 gelatine leaves

lemon juice

fresh berries

Boil the sugar and water together with the lemon which should be cut in half and reduce to 750ml of stock syrup. Add the gelatine leaves and Sauternes to the stock syrup. Check for sweetness; add a touch more lemon juice should it be required.

Place the jelly in a mould just to cover the bottom. Leave to set then add a selection of berries and cover with more liquid jelly, leave to set. Continue this method until the mould is full. Chill in the fridge for 2-3 hours until ready to serve.

CRATHORNE HALL

Ian Samson

Seared hand-dived scallops with lobster risotto and saffron nage

serves 4

Hand-dived scallops are literally handpicked by a diver from the bottom of the seabed, for their cleaner, fresher taste. Most scallops are dredged by machine and can collect a lot of grit and sand. Both are available from a good fishmonger

for the risotto

8 hand-dived scallops

250g Vialone Nano risotto rice

50g unsalted butter

40g olive oil

half a fresh bay leaf

1 sprig of rosemary

10g garlic

200g rocket leaves - roughly chopped

50g Regianno Parmesan

65ml Vermouth

5g salt, white pepper, cayenne pepper mixed

300g diced lobster meat

200g lobster meat as 4 clean chunks for slicing

1 litre white chicken stock

For the saffron nage (light stock based sauce)

250 ml chicken stock

250 ml fish stock

400 ml double cream

2g saffron strands

200g unsalted butter

5g salt and pepper mix

20g diced chicken fillet trimmings (bones, skin and wings)

20g diced white fish trimmings (bones and skin)

100 ml dry Vermouth

5g dill tips

12 asparagus tips, blanched

In a thick-bottomed pan, gently heat the olive oil, butter, bay leaf and rosemary. Once the butter starts to foam, add the risotto rice and fry gently, coating every grain. Warm the chicken stock. Stir in half the Vermouth into the rice. Keep stirring in the stock one ladle at a time whilst it is being absorbed by the rice. When all the stock has been used, the risotto will still be quite wet and you will need to keep it on the heat for about another 5 minutes. Season, stir in the Parmesan, the rest of the Vermouth, the diced lobster meat and the roughly chopped rocket and spinach. Leave at the side of the stove and it will thicken slightly and stay hot. Take the 4 pieces of lobster and slice thinly, season and brush with a little olive oil and leave to warm.

For the saffron nage sauce, sweat the chicken and fish trimmings in a little olive oil. Add the saffron strands and the Vermouth. Reduce by half and then add the chicken and fish stocks and reduce further until sticky in consistency. Add the cream and bring to simmering point and remove from the heat. Crush the dill tips and infuse for 15 minutes and pass the whole sauce through a fine muslin cloth or fine sieve. Next take the scallops and slice each of them evenly into 3 pieces. In a non-stick pan, fry them in a little olive oil until they are a rich caramelised golden colour on each side. Season and

remove from the pan and de-glaze with lemon juice. Add this to the nage but keep the scallops aside to keep warm.

To serve, arrange the 4 plates with ring cutters for the risotto on each one. Put 4 even amounts of risotto in each and press down. It should be firm enough to hold but soft and wet when it's spooned. Arrange the scallops in a neat ring round the top of the risotto and the lobster slice opposite. To the right hand side place 3 asparagus tips neatly, tip to tail. Warm the nage and blitz in the butter using a hand blender for a frothy effect. Spoon the froth over the asparagus and round the risotto. Remove the rings and add the four springs of chervil for a garnish and serve.

Pot-roast squab pigeon with apple choucroute, foie gras, white grape and vanilla jus

serves 4

for the choucroute

1 small white cabbage, very thinly sliced

100 ml white wine

100 white wine vinegar

4 juniper berries

1 sprig of rosemary

1 sprig of thyme

200 ml chicken stock

100 ml apple juice

100 ml sweet cider

125g unsalted butter

for the fondant potato

4 baking potatoes

100ml veal (or chicken) stock

120g butter

50ml olive oil

2 garlic cloves

1 sprig of thyme

1 bay leaf

for the jus

600 ml brown chicken stock

100g pigeon trimmings

1 sprig of marjoram

1 sprig rosemary

1 vanilla pod - seeds separate

50g unsalted butter

all the following need to soak together for 8 hours:

60g white raisins - available from health food shops

150ml Armagnac

50ml stock syrup - available from good supermarkets

for the pigeons

4 squab (corn-fed) pigeons

20g rosemary

50g unsalted butter

10 cloves garlic

250ml red wine

250ml chicken stock

50g thyme

4 x 80g slices of foie gras

4 slices of brioche half an inch thick

100 ml olive oil

50g unsalted butter

150g Girolles mushrooms, cleaned and trimmed

half a lemon

Starting with the choucroute, melt the butter in a thick-bottomed pan until it begins to bubble and then add the cabbage and stir. Add all the stock, apple juice, cider, wine, vinegar, juniper berries and herbs. Stir well, cover with a sheet of silicon paper and cook for 2 hours over a medium to low heat, stirring occasionally. Keep checking that the liquid does not evaporate too quickly, if it does, reduce the heat and top up with warm apple juice or cider. When the cabbage is soft and tender, season, drain off any liquid, (there shouldn't be much left) and keep warm.

Next, take the pigeons and trim off the wings and remove the offal. Rinse and pat dry with kitchen paper. Seal the pigeon in a hot pan with olive oil and butter, colouring well to a deep brown. Remove each pigeon, discard the oil and individually cover in butter paper or silicon paper. De-glaze the pan with the red wine and chicken stock and add the rosemary and thyme, bring to the boil and then add the pigeons. Cook for 12 minutes in an oven at approximately 200°C/Gas Mark 6. Remove and rest upside down in a clean tray and keep warm. Pass the remaining liquid through a muslin cloth or fine sieve and then reduce by half.

For the fondant potatoes, cut each potato in a barrel shape using a cutter. Trim with a small knife, to give 4 even barrels. Pan-fry in the oil and butter until golden. Add the veal stock and braise in the oven at 200°C/Gas Mark 6 until just cooked, this should take approximately 40-45 minutes. Remove the potatoes from the stock and reduce it until it is sticky and then return the potatoes and coat in the sauce. Keep them warm until required. Cut the brioche slices into croûtons using a heart shaped cutter, if you have one. If not, a neat square will do. Pan-fry in the oil and butter until both sides are golden and keep warm. Pan-fry the Girolle mushrooms in a little

olive oil and butter gently for 4-5 minutes. Season well and squeeze a little lemon juice onto them. Drain and keep warm. Fry the pigeon wings and add the chicken stock, marjoram and vanilla pod. Reduce by half and add the butter, season and pass through a fine sieve and keep warm. Stir in the vanilla seeds and marinated raisins at the last minute. Re-heat, adjust the seasoning and keep warm.

To serve, assemble the fondant potato at the top of each plate at 11 o'clock and at 5 o'clock using a small cutter, place even amounts of choucroute into the ring, pressing down to give a cylindrical shape. Leave the cutter on for a moment. Place the croûton at 8 o'clock using a little potato purée to hold it in place. Remove the legs from the pigeon and then the thighbone from that, season and pile onto the

croûton. Remove the breast from the carcass, season and place on top of the legs to form a neat heart shape. Fry the foie gras in a hot pan, season well and cook until caramelised and dark in colour. Season and finish on the top of the choucroute. Remove the rings and scatter the Girolles round the plate, evenly but not too neatly, and finally drizzle the sauce over and around the pigeon and garnish with a little chervil and serve.

Croustillant of apple and fig with vanilla ice cream and cinnamon syrup

serves 4

for the croustillant

12 won ton sheets

1 egg yolk

4 Granny Smith apples

4 blue figs

8 raspberries, soaked in raspberry vinegar and stock syrup

10g cinnamon

50g butter

50g icing sugar

for the cinnamon syrup

100 ml stock syrup

half a cinnamon stick

2 cloves

1 star anise crushed

half a vanilla pod

for the apple crisps

3 Granny Smith Apples

stock syrup

icing sugar

for the ice cream

4 quenelles of good quality vanilla ice cream

Start by making the apple crisps. Slice the apples finely, ideally on a mandolin. Dip into the syrup and place onto a non-stick baking tray. Dry in a low oven at about 100°C/Gas Mark 1/2 until crisp, dust with icing sugar and caramelise until golden with a blow torch or under the grill. Peel the apples, core and cut into small dice. Dice the figs and sauté both together in the butter, add the sugar and cinnamon and cook slowly on a very low heat or at the side of the stove until the mix resembles a chutney consistency and then allow to cool. Spoon a teaspoon of the mixture into the centre of 6 won ton sheet and brush egg yolk round the edges and neatly place a sheet on top and shape into a parcel. Trim off the edges to make a neat square.

Add all the syrup ingredients together and simmer for 5 minutes. Pass through a fine sieve and leave to cool. Warm the vegetable oil up to 180°C and deep fry the won tons in the oil until golden in colour and drain on kitchen paper, season with caster sugar and keep warm but not too hot. With a little whipped cream, layer the three won tons per person with the apple crisps to form a tower of won ton and apple crisps. Dust with icing sugar and arrange on the plate at 9 o'clock. Allowing 4 raspberries per person, drain well and place them in a line from top to bottom on the plate. Finally make the ice cream quenelles with 2 dessertspoons and arrange neatly opposite the tower and drizzle the syrup on the plate and garnish with a few mint sprigs.

CALLOW HALL

Anthony Spencer

Baked sea bass parcel with crispy leeks and prawns, lime and coriander dressing

serves 4

1 small packet of filo pastry

2 x 170g fillets of sea bass, scaled with pin bones removed

1 medium sized leek

175g Royal Greenland prawns

for the dressing

3 limes

1 red chilli, de-seeded and finely chopped

1 green chilli, de-seeded and finely chopped

20g stem of ginger, finely chopped

15ml of the sugar syrup from the stem ginger

10ml Chinese fish sauce, Blue Dragon or similar

1 clove of garlic, squeezed through a garlic press

2 bunches of fresh coriander, roughly chopped

10ml sesame oil

120ml olive oil
(Pumace or similar, though not extra virgin; to be totally authentic you should use sunflower oil.)

salt to taste.

Remove the top of the leek, as it is too tough and bitter to use in this dish, but wash and use in the lamb stock for the next course. Shred the rest of the leek into very fine 2" lengths. Wash, drain and mix with the defrosted prawns.

Zest and juice the limes into a bowl and add the chillies, ginger, garlic and fresh coriander. Mix together with the rest of the ingredients for a very fresh tasting dressing. Mix a good 3 tablespoons with the leek and prawns and reserve the rest.

To make the parcel, lay out a sheet of filo pastry and cut in half (ideally you will end up with a piece approx 15cm x 20cm). Brush half of this with the vegetable/sesame oil and fold in half to make a double layer. Place half of the sea bass fillet, skin-side down in the middle, season to taste and place a little of the leek and prawns on top. Fold over the sides of the filo, then the ends to make a parcel, sticking it together with a little more oil. Turn the whole parcel over so the folds are underneath and place on baking paper on a baking tray. Bake for approximately 8 minutes at 200°C/Gas Mark 6.

To serve place a pile of leeks and prawns in the centre of the plate, place the parcel on top, stir up your dressing and drizzle around.

Roast loin of lamb Moroccan style with couscous farce and rosemary jus

serves 8

2 boned rolled loins of lamb

250g couscous

3 peppers (1 red, 1 yellow, 1 green)

1 aubergine

olive oil

12 x ¹/₂ sundried tomatoes in oil

approx 2 litres good lamb stock

¹/₂ bottle (37.5cl) red wine

2 dessertspoons of honey

25g butter

1 large onion

40g caster sugar

1 bunch fresh rosemary

1 small tin harissa
(Moroccan chilli paste)

1 teaspoon tomato purée paste

2 cloves of garlic, pressed and mixed
with maldon or similar sea salt

De-seed and slice the peppers into baton sized pieces. Put into a roasting tray with some rosemary leaves taken from the stem, drizzle with olive oil, season and put in a medium oven until lightly roasted for approximately 20 minutes, turning occasionally. Similarly, slice the aubergine into baton pieces and put on a roasting tray, drizzle with olive oil (not too much as aubergine acts like a sponge), season and place under a hot grill, turning until gently browned.

Chop some rosemary and mix with the cous cous. To 400ml boiling water add ¹/₂ teaspoon salt, 1 tablespoon olive oil, ¹/₂ teaspoon of harissa and the teaspoon of tomato purée. Add the couscous and rosemary, cover and leave standing for 5 minutes. Add the butter or substitute for the same amount of olive oil if you prefer and stir until the grains are separated with a fork. Chop up the sun dried tomatoes and leaving 4 to garnish, add to the couscous with the pepper and aubergine, likewise reserving a little for garnishing. Allow couscous to cool.

To make the sauce add the wine to the lamb stock and boil to reduce. At the same time in a good old-fashioned black iron pan, brown the onion (very brown but not black) with a little vegetable oil over a moderate heat. When very brown turn up the heat and add the sugar until you have onion caramel. Add to the reducing stock and wine. Add the honey and some rosemary, a good knob of butter and just a little salt and pepper. Reduce until you have about 1 pint of sauce remaining and strain through a fine sieve.

Unroll the rolled lamb loins, trim out any fatty bits and cut half way under between the eye of the meat and the fat. Place your couscous stuffing along here and roll up again tightly. Tie with string along the length of the loin. Rub with the garlic salt and harissa paste. Go easy on the harissa – it is very strong and would suggest using a rubber glove or just wrap your hand in cling film for this part of the procedure. Roast the lamb in a hot oven 200˚C/Gas Mark 6 for 15 to 20 minutes and allow to rest.

To serve, cut the lamb into slices and arrange on the plate. Garnish with remaining aubergine, pepper, tomato and a sprig of rosemary and the sauce.

Bread & almond pudding with vanilla pod ice cream and crème anglaise

serves 4

Separate 1 egg. Mix the white with the marzipan to form a paste. Mix the other 4 whole eggs plus the 1 yolk with the sugar then add the milk and cream. Cut out 8 circles of bread and spread with marzipan paste. Butter the ramekin dishes and place 1 circle of bread in the bottom, almond side up. Fill up with the egg mixture (any remaining paste can be mixed into the egg/milk/cream depending on the sweetness of your tooth). Top with a second bread circle, almond side down on top, press down under the egg mixture and sprinkle with a little ground nutmeg. Bake in a bain-marie, (low sided roasting tin, half filled with water) in a medium oven 145°C/Gas Mark 1½ until the custard has set, though not boiled, approximately half an hour to 45 minutes. Remove and allow to cool.

Slice the vanilla pod down its length and scrape the seeds into the milk and cream, put the split pod in too. In a bowl mix the egg yolks and the sugar. Heat the milk & cream in a saucepan but do not boil. Pour the hot milk onto the egg/sugar whilst whisking, then strain back into the clean pan.

Over a low heat stir the custard mix systematically across the bottom and round the sides with a wooden spoon, so that it does not 'catch'. When the custard coats the back of the spoon and you can draw your finger through the custard leaving a line on the back of the spoon the custard is ready.

For those with a thermometer this is approx 86-88°C. Do not boil otherwise splitting will occur. Allow to cool.

Reserve a little of the custard mix for use as the crème anglaise, adding the dash of Amaretto. The main part, churn in an ice cream machine if you have one. If not place in a bowl in the freezer and stir regularly, about every hour until you have your ice cream. Or there's always Häagen Dazs!

To serve run a knife around the edge of the ramekins and tip out the puddings. They can be served cold, but are much nicer if you warm them with steam or in the oven. Serve with the crème anglais and a scoop of ice cream.

for the bread and almond pudding

5 eggs, medium size

125g white marzipan paste

²/3pt milk

¹/3pt cream

85g caster sugar

4 very thin slices good quality white bread (bakers white tin loaf)

a little melted butter

ground nutmeg

4 x 4¹/2 fl oz ramekin dishes

for the vanilla pod ice cream & crème anglais

100ml egg yolk (approx 6 egg yolks)

570ml milk

290ml cream

170g caster sugar

1 vanilla pod

a dash of Amaretto

CREWE HALL

Jonathan File

Confit of lamb with wild mushrooms, parsley and tomatoes finished with a cassis jus and roasted garlic

serves 4

600g piece shoulder of lamb

6 chopped shallots

2 cloves chopped garlic

rock salt

whole peppercorns

2 sprigs rosemary

2 sprigs thyme

1 litre duck/goose fat

4 shallots, finely diced

4 plum tomatoes, skinned, deseeded and cut into $^1/_2$cm squares

100g mixed wild mushrooms

$^1/_2$ bunch of parsley, finely chopped

juice of 1 lemon

for the potato galette

1 potato, cut into very fine strips

knob of butter

salt and pepper

for the roasted garlic

12 cloves of garlic, unpeeled

for the cassis jus

1 litre good beef stock

200ml red wine

4 shallots, chopped

2 cloves garlic, chopped

150ml cassis

chervil to garnish

For the lamb confit, dry marinade the lamb by placing in a sealed container with the chopped shallots, garlic, rosemary and thyme. Leave refrigerated for 2 days. Remove the lamb, rinse and pat dry with kitchen paper. Place the shoulder of lamb into a thick-bottomed pan and cover with duck/goose fat. Cook on a very low heat for around 5 hours, until the meat breaks down completely. Remove the lamb from the fat.

For the potato galette, take the fine strips of potato and cook in butter in a galette tin to create a wafer-like disk. Make 2 disks for each person.

Roast the whole garlic cloves in a little oil in a hot oven and leave to one side.

For the cassis jus, fry off the garlic and shallots. Add the red wine and reduce by three-quarters. Add the beef stock and reduce by half. Separately reduce the cassis by half and then add to the stock.

Warm a thick-bottomed pan on the stove. Add a little of the cooking fat from the lamb. Fry off the shallots and wild mushrooms until a light golden colour is achieved. Return the shoulder of lamb and fry off. This will cause the lamb to break right down to fine strips. Add the parsley and tomatoes and warm through. Season with lemon juice, salt and pepper.

To serve, place 1 of the potato galettes in the centre of the plate. Spoon the lamb confit mixture into a ring on top of the galette, top with the second galette. Place 3 cloves of roasted garlic evenly around the lamb and dress the plate with the cassis jus. Garnish with sprigs of chervil.

Roasted fillet of sea bass set on a pink peppercorn and black pudding mash dressed with a balsamic syrup and rocket oil

serves 4

4 small fillets of sea bass, scaled and pin boned

800g potatoes, peeled and chopped

60g unsalted butter

2 egg yolks

2tsp pink peppercorns

120g Bury black pudding, diced into $^1/2$cm squares

20g chopped rocket

for the balsamic syrup

500ml aged balsamic vinegar

50g caster sugar

for the rocket oil

500g rocket

75ml olive oil

75ml sunflower oil

Cook the diced potatoes in lightly salted water until soft. Drain and leave on the heat for a few minutes to thoroughly dry them out. Add the butter and egg yolks. Mash and leave to one side. Fry the diced black pudding and add to the mashed potatoes, add the peppercorns and chopped rocket.

For the balsamic syrup, place the vinegar and sugar in a thick-bottomed pan, bring to the boil and reduce by three-quarters, leave to one side.

For the rocket oil, place the rocket, olive and sunflower oil in a blender and liquidise, pass through a very fine sieve and leave to one side.

Pan fry the bass in a little oil. Place the skin-side down and cook until the skin has coloured and become crispy. Gently turn over and finish cooking. The bass will be cooked in about 4 minutes.

To serve, place the black pudding mashed potatoes in the centre of the plate, top with the bass and drizzle the Balsamic syrup and rocket oil around the plate.

Rich dark chocolate torte with Guinness ice cream and white chocolate sauce

serves 4

500g dark, plain chocolate

50g glucose

500g double cream

for the ice cream

750ml double cream

750ml draft Guinness

600ml water

500g sugar

10 egg yolks

for the white chocolate sauce

500g white chocolate

375ml milk

75ml double cream

75g sugar

75g butter

Boil the double cream and sugar together; pour over the dark chocolate and glucose. Mix until all the chocolate has dissolved and pour into 4 separate rings.

For the ice cream, boil the cream and Guinness together and leave to one side. Place the egg yolks in a mixing machine and whisk at high speed until they thicken and treble in size. Boil the water and sugar together to the 'soft ball' stage (120°C). When the sugar is ready, pour slowly onto the egg yolks whilst they are still whisking in the machine, continue to mix until cool.

Add the cream and Guinness mixture to the egg and sugar, cool and churn in a conventional ice-cream machine.

For the chocolate sauce, boil the milk, cream and sugar together then pour on to the white chocolate, finally stir in the butter. Stir occasionally until the sauce is cold to prevent the butter splitting in the sauce.

To serve, dust the top of the torte with cocoa powder and mark with a knife, place the torte to one side of the plate; arrange the ice cream on a tuille biscuit and dress with the sauce.

THE GIBBON BRIDGE HOTEL

Gary Buxton

Lobster, langoustine and scallop terrine

serves 4

for the shellfish stock

1kg shellfish bones

the following for the braised vegetables or mirepoix

the green part of two leeks, chopped

1 carrot, peeled and roughly diced

1 clove of garlic

1 bay leaf

6 shallots, peeled and sliced

1 stick of celery

2 tablespoons tomato purée

1/2cup of brandy

2.85 litres of water

1/2cup of red wine

for the clarification

4 egg whites

1 stick of celery

8 leaves of gelatine

for the filling

1/2 cooked lobster

8 cooked languistine

4 scallops, sliced into 3 or 4 pieces

1 long slice of smoked salmon, finely shredded

1/4 each of red, green and yellow pepper, finely chopped

for the dressing

100ml of olive oil

4 lavender flower stems

1/4 of each red, green and yellow pepper, finely chopped

for the garnish

lettuce

2 whole langoustine

To start, make the shellfish stock by placing all the bones in a tray and roasting them in the oven for 20 minutes on 225°C/Gas Mark 9, just to slightly colour them. Meanwhile sweat off the mireopoix of vegetables until soft and add the tomato purée and the roasted bones. Next add the brandy and the red wine and flame it to cook off the alcohol. Add the water, bring to the boil and then simmer for at least 2 hours, topping up with more water when necessary. Pass through a fine sieve and chill.

To clarify the stock, blitz the stick of celery with the four egg whites in a food processor and add to the cool stock in a pan. Cook over a medium heat, making sure it doesn't boil. At this stage you should see a frothy crust developing on the surface. Once the stock has clarified, sieve it through a muslin cloth, which should leave it looking very clear. Now reduce the stock to about 570ml whilst soaking the gelatine in a little water. Once soaked, squeeze out the excess water and add to the hot stock. Line a 450g terrine or 1 pint individual mould with cling film and build up layer by layer with the shellfish, stock and pepper. Keep in the fridge until needed.

For the dressing, lightly warm the olive oil and add the lavender flowers and diced peppers and leave to infuse.

To serve, take a slice of terrine and place on a plate. Garnish with picked lettuce and drizzle the dressing over the leaves and around the plate.

Loin of lamb in filo pastry

serves 4

4 racks of lamb with 4 bones each

1 tablespoon grain mustard

4 sheets filo pastry

150ml clarified butter

2 roasted peppers, cut into 1" discs

for the braised lentils

1 onion, finely diced

1 clove of garlic, finely chopped

100g lentils

425ml chicken stock

4 sprigs of rosemary, finely chopped

for the mint and parsley oil

blitz all the following ingredients together in a food processor and strain

150ml olive oil

1 handful of mint

1 handful of parsley

for the sauce

200ml veal stock

1/2 teaspoon grain mustard

1/2 teaspoon green peppercorns

for the quenelles of mash potato

2 large Maris Piper potatoes

1/4 teaspoon salt

1 tablespoon double cream

knob of butter

pinch of pepper

1/2 tablespoon chopped chives

1/2 tablespoon chopped chervil

for the garnish

12 baby carrots

4 quenelles of herb mash potato

Wash and peel the potato and cut into eight even sized pieces. Place in a pan of water with the salt and bring to the boil. Simmer until you can see the potato just starting to break up. Strain off the water and return to the pan over a low heat to dry them off. Mash the potatoes with the cream, butter, pepper and herbs. Check the seasoning and keep warm until required.

Prepare the lamb by removing the bones and any excess fat and sinew. Seal on all sides in a very hot pan. Remove immediately and coat the lamb in the grain mustard and leave to cool. Next take the sheets of filo pastry and brush them with butter and individually wrap each piece of lamb with one sheet of pastry. Put the lamb on a tray, large enough for them to brown evenly during cooking and place in the oven at 230°C/Gas Mark 8 for 12-15

minutes for pink, or a little longer for a more 'well done' result. Meanwhile, cook the lentils by firstly sweating off the onions and garlic. Add the lentils and chicken stock and cook for 15-20 minutes until just tender. By now the lamb should be cooked and allowed to relax for 10 minutes.

To make the sauce, bring all the ingredients to the boil and keep warm until needed.

To serve, slice the lamb diagonally and stand on the flat ends. Take a ring and layer up the lentils and red pepper until you have three layers. Now drizzle a little of the green peppercorn sauce and the mint and parsley oil around the plate and garnish with 3 carrots. Mould the quenelle of mash potato between two tablespoons and arrange on the plate.

Orchard of Amaretto sabayon

serves 4

1 pear

1 apple

1 nectarine

2 plums

1 peach

cherries

juice of 1 lemon

for the sabayon

2 whole eggs

100g caster sugar

2 tablespoons Amaretto

50g mascarpone cheese

Wash all the fruit, removing any stones or seeds and cut into quarters, (except the cherries). Slice the fruit as thinly as possible and arrange in a bowl. Squeeze a little lemon juice over the top to stop discolouration and set aside. To prepare the sabayon, crack the eggs in a glass bowl, add the sugar and Amaretto and whisk gently over a pan of hot water until it becomes thick and white in colour. Remove from the pan and fold in the mascarpone.

To serve, arrange the fruits on individual plates in a fan shape. Spoon the sabayon over the fruit. Place under the grill or use a blowtorch to lightly brown the top. Dust with icing sugar and garnish with fresh cherries. This can be put together prior to sitting down to dinner.

CASHEL PALACE HOTEL

Declan Hayes

Courgette, roasted red pepper and sesame goats cheese tartlet served with frizzy leaf salad

serves 4

1 medium red pepper,
roasted and peeled

1 garlic clove

1 medium clove

1 tablespoon olive oil

80g goats cheese

5g sesame seeds, toasted

for the pastry

80g plain flour

pinch of salt

40g of butter

20ml cold water

1 tablespoon basil, chopped

freshly ground pepper

To make the pastry, sift the flour, pepper and salt. Add the butter in cubes and mix to a breadcrumb mixture. Make a well in the centre and add the water and basil. When it comes together, knead briefly. Chill for 20 minutes. Roll out on a floured surface to $1/8$" thick. Roll the pastry over 4 individual pastry cases and prick the bottoms with a fork. Bake blind for 5 minutes at 180°C/Gas Mark 4.

Chop the courgette and garlic and sauté in the olive oil for 5 minutes without colouring. Do the same for the red pepper and leave to rest. Place a layer of the red pepper on the bottom of each baked tartlet, then add the courgette and top with a slice of goats cheese. Sprinkle with toasted sesame seeds and bake in the oven at 180°C for 6 – 8 minutes.

To serve, place 1 tartlet on each plate. On top of each place a fan of red pepper and courgette. Dress the plate with some mustard seed vinaigrette, then place a spear of frizzy lettuce wrapped in carrot curls alongside each tartlet.

Fillet of beef with roasted ginger apple, spaghetti of vegetables, black pepper Parmesan tuiles, oregano and sun-dried tomato sauce

serves 4

4 x 200g beef fillets

salt and black pepper

1 tablespoon olive oil

40g spaghetti of vegetables
(courgette, leek and carrot)

40g fresh Parmesan

freshly ground black pepper

60g red apples

crystallized ginger

for the apples

8 slices of golden delicious red apples

8 slices crystallized ginger

for the sauce

80g sun-dried tomatoes in olive oil

80g very ripe fresh tomatoes

100ml chicken stock

20ml balsamic vinegar

2 tablespoons fresh oregano leaves,
finely chopped

salt and freshly ground pepper

for the oregano oil

30ml extra virgin oil

10g fresh oregano leaves

seasoning

For the apples, heat a smoking hot pan, add the apple and lightly brown on both sides. Place in the oven with grated ginger on top. Cook for 5 minutes 200°C/Gas Mark 6.

To make the sauce, combine all the tomatoes, chicken stock and balsamic vinegar in a food processor. Buzz for 2 minutes, then strain through a fine sieve into a bowl. Leave to one side.

For the oregano oil, place the oil, oregano and seasoning in a food processor and buzz for 2 minutes. Place in a bowl and leave to one side.

To make the spaghetti of vegetables, peel the carrot and courgette and cut into fine julienne strips. Do the same for the leek using the white part only and remove the centre stalk. Set aside in a bowl.

To make the black pepper Parmesan tuiles, heat a large frying pan and place 8 ring cutters into it. Grate 40g of fresh Parmesan and add fresh black pepper. Place equal amounts into each ring cutter. Cook for 3-5 minutes. When cooked place the pan in a tray of iced water. When cool, remove and set aside.

Preheat the oven to 200°C/Gas Mark 6. Season the fillets and sear on both sides in a smoking hot pan. Place in the oven and cook to your liking.

To serve, lay 4 hot plates on a worktop. Place 2 apple slices on each plate. Put a beef fillet on top. Then put the spaghetti of vegetables sautéed in butter on top of that. Finally place the tuiles on each one. Pour the cold sauce in a ribbon around the fillets and then sprinkle with a few drops of basil oil.

Warm pear and ginger brandy snap basket served with vanilla ice cream and orange and Amaretto sauce

serves 4

$^1/_2$ litre stock syrup

2 vanilla pods

3 star anise

4 ripe Comice pears

for the brandy ginger snap baskets

65g of butter

120g caster sugar

60g flour, soft

60g golden syrup

2 pieces of crystallised ginger

for the orange, mango and Amaretto sauce

300ml orange juice made from Spanish or Moroccan oranges and sieved

30g caster sugar

1 orange, peeled and segmented

5ml Amaretto

To poach the pears, peel neatly and place in a pot just big enough to hold them. Completely cover with stock syrup and poke in the star anise and vanilla pods. Place some parchment paper over the top and gently poach for 20 – 25 minutes.

To make the brandy ginger snap baskets, combine the butter and sugar in a bowl and beat. Then add the golden syrup, grated crystallised ginger, whisk and add the sieved flour. Place in a fridge for 20 minutes. Put four portions of 30g each of the mixture four inches apart on an oiled baking tray and bake at 200°C/Gas Mark 6 for 5 minutes until brown. Place 4 tart moulds 2"

in diameter upside down. When the mixture is slightly cool, place over the moulds and shape into baskets.

To make the sauce, place the orange segments in a pan with the Amaretto and reduce. Add the sugar and orange juice and reduce by two thirds. Use accordingly.

To serve, place a tuile on each plate. Halve the pears and put a half into each basket. Then neatly fan the other half in front. Serve with a good quality ice cream. Drizzle the plate lightly with the Amaretto and orange sauce, then fan 3 suprêmes of orange to the side of the basket with raspberry coulis in between and lightly dust with icing sugar.

ASHDOWN PARK

John McManus

Lobster and crab tian with Thai spices

serves 4

1 red pepper

2 x 450g cooked lobsters

3 tablespoons fish stock

175ml coconut milk

1 gelatine leaf

150ml double cream, whipped

280g fresh white crab meat

1 tablespoon chopped fresh coriander

4 spring onions, finely sliced

a squeeze of lime juice

1 tablespoon crème fraîche

salt and freshly ground black pepper

To garnish

12-16 Thai asparagus spears

4 long chives

8 peeled cooked tiger prawns

a few leaves of curly endive, lightly dressed

Roast the red pepper under the grill or in a hot oven until blistered all over. Peel and deseed it, then cut out 4 discs with a 6cm cutter. Set aside.

Remove the meat from the lobsters. Place half of it in a food processor, add 2 tablespoons of the fish stock and half the coconut milk and process for 1 minute. Strain through a fine sieve into a bowl.

Soak the gelatine in cold water for 5 minutes, then drain. Put the remaining fish stock in a small pan, add the gelatine and heat gently until dissolved. Stir it into the lobster mixture and then fold in the whipped cream. Season to taste.

Dice the remaining lobster meat and divide it between four 6cm metal rings, placed on a tray. Spoon the lobster mousse on top of the meat, filling the rings half way. Chill for 30 minutes or until set.

Remove any pieces of shell from the crab meat and place it in a bowl. Bind with the rest of the coconut milk, then stir in the chopped coriander, spring onions, lime juice and crème fraîche. Place the crab mixture on top of the lobster mousse and top with the roasted pepper discs.

For the garnish, cook the asparagus in boiling salted water until just tender, then drain and refresh in cold water. Drain again, divide into 4 bundles and tie each one with a chive.

To serve, run a knife round the edge of each mould and turn out on to 4 plates. Garnish with the Thai asparagus, prawns and curly endive.

Saddle of lamb with spinach mousse, baby vegetables and goats cheese sauce

serves 4

1 saddle of lamb
(ask your butcher to take it off the bone and tie it into 2 rolls)

salt and freshly ground black pepper

For the spinach mousse

280g fresh spinach, trimmed

1 teaspoon butter

1 small garlic clove, peeled but left whole

175ml double cream

2 egg yolks

For the goat's cheese sauce

150ml good-quality lamb stock

4 tablespoons double cream

25g Golden Cross goat's cheese

For the baby vegetables

about 50g each of your favourites, eg carrots, leeks, turnips etc

First make the spinach mousse. Put the spinach into a large pan of boiling water and cook for 1 minute, then drain thoroughly. Melt the butter in a pan, add the garlic clove and spinach and sauté for 2 minutes. Remove the garlic, then add the cream and some seasoning. Simmer until the cream has reduced slightly. Transfer the mixture to a food processor, add the egg yolks and process until smooth. Check the seasoning and then pour into 4 buttered dariole moulds. Put the moulds in an earthenware dish, with a piece of folded kitchen paper under each one. Pour water into the dish so that it is about 2cm deep. Cook in an oven preheated to 160°C/Gas Mark 3 for 25 minutes, then remove and set aside.

Meanwhile, make the cheese sauce. Boil the lamb stock in a pan until reduced by about a third. Add the cream and bring back to the boil, then remove from the heat, add the goat's cheese and whisk to melt the cheese. Strain the mixture through a fine sieve into a small pan.

Lightly cook the baby vegetables in boiling salted water until tender, then drain and set aside.

Season the lamb, place on a roasting tray and cook in an oven preheated to 200°C/Gas Mark 6 for 3 minutes. Turn and cook for another 3 minutes. Remove from the oven and leave to rest for 5 minutes.

Slice each roll into 6 pieces. Place 3 slices on each serving plate, then turn out the spinach mousse and place on each plate. Garnish with the baby vegetables, pour over the goat's cheese sauce and serve.

Orange treacle sponge

serves 4

100g unsalted butter

100g caster sugar

1 large egg

zest and juice of 1 orange

100g self-raising flour

1 tablespoon orange liqueur

4 tablespoons golden syrup

For the caramelised orange compôte and crystallised orange zest

3 oranges

100g caster sugar, plus extra to coat

For the crème anglaise:

4 egg yolks

85g caster sugar

¹/2 vanilla pod

330ml milk

First prepare the orange compôte and crystallised zest. Remove the zest from the oranges and cut it into fine julienne strips. Put half the sugar in a small pan with a tablespoon of water and heat until dissolved, then boil until it reaches 116°C on a sugar thermometer. Add the orange zest and cook for 2-3 minutes.

Meanwhile, spread some sugar out on a small tray. Using 2 forks, remove the orange zest from the pan and put it in the tray of sugar. Toss until the strands are separated and well coated in sugar. Store in an airtight tin (you won't need it all for this recipe but it will keep for a week or so).

For the compôte, squeeze the juice from one of the oranges and set aside. Peel the other 2 oranges, removing all the white pith, and take out the segments. Dissolve the remaining 50g sugar in a tablespoon of water and then boil until it reaches 116°C. Stir in the juice, then add the orange segments and remove from the heat. Leave to cool.

To make the crème anglaise, beat the egg yolks and sugar together until smooth. Split open the vanilla pod lengthways and scrape out the seeds, then put the pod and seeds in a pan with the milk and bring to boiling point. Pour the milk on to the egg yolk mixture, stirring all the time, then return it to the pan and cook over a low heat until it thickens enough to coat the back of the spoon (do not let it boil). Strain through a fine sieve into a bowl.

For the orange treacle sponge, cream the butter until pale and fluffy, then beat in the caster sugar. Gradually beat in the egg, followed by the orange zest and juice. Sift in the flour and fold it in, then stir in the liqueur.

Butter 4 dariole moulds and sprinkle them lightly with sugar. Line the base of each one with a small circle of baking parchment. Put a tablespoon of golden syrup in the bottom of each mould and top up with the pudding mix. Put another piece of greaseproof paper on the top. Put the moulds in an ovenproof dish containing 1.5cm water and cover with foil. Bake in an oven preheated to 180°C/Gas Mark 4 for 50 minutes or until golden.

To serve, gently warm the compote and the crème anglaise. Pour the sauce into 4 shallow bowls, then turn out a pudding into each bowl, removing the baking parchment. Spoon the warm compote on top of the puddings and garnish with a little crystallised orange zest.

NUTFIELD PRIORY

David Evans

Seared galette of scallops with choron sauce and scallop mousseline

serves 4

12 large scallops, in the shell

1kg potatoes, Maris Piper or Wares

500g unsalted butter

20ml double cream

500g shallots

3 cloves garlic, peeled

1 leek

1 lemon

20ml dry white wine

1 tablespoon white wine vinegar

1 tomato

2 eggs, separated

sea salt

milled pepper

a pinch of cayenne pepper

small bunch of chives

1 bay leaf

small bunch of thyme

Wash and peel the potatoes and cut into cylinders approximately 4cms in diameter. Slice the cylinders into roundelles/slices 5mm thick. Peel the shallots. Thinly slice 2 of them into circles and finely chop the remainder with the garlic. Cut a 20cm length from the centre of the leek, cut in half lengthways and wash thoroughly. Skin the tomatoes, remove the seeds and cut into fine, uniform dice. Finely chop the chives and shred the bay leaf.

Carefully remove the scallops from their shells – clean, trim and wash thoroughly. Remove the roes and purée with 4 whole scallops and the egg white. Pass the mixture through a fine sieve. Slice each of the remaining scallops into 4 roundelles. Heavily butter 4 squares of greaseproof paper and overlap 7 roundelles/slices in a pinwheel style and place 1 slice in the centre. Season with sea salt and pepper and place each paper onto a side plate, cover with clingfilm and refrigerate.

For the Anna potatoes, sweat off the drained potato slices in 100gms butter until they feel sticky. Butter 4 non-stick 15cm sauté pans or timbales. Place 1 potato slice in the centre and carefully overlap some other slices onto the centre piece. Season with salt and pepper and repeat with another layer. Cover with a buttered piece of greaseproof paper and cook in the oven at 160°C/Gas Mark 1^1/$_2$ for 30-40minutes, until the base is golden brown and crisp. (A gentle weight on top of each potato galette will ensure good adhesion of the individual pieces).

For the confit of shallot, sweat off the finely chopped shallots and garlic. Add the white wine and boil until emulsified. Add the grated lemon zest and juice, the bay leaf and 2 sprigs of thyme. Cook gently for 7-8 minutes, until most of the liquid has evaporated.

For the scallop mousse, put the scallop purée into a bowl over ice and gradually beat in the cream. Season with salt and cayenne pepper.

Blanch the strips of leeks until soft. Line a small terrine mould with clingfilm. Carefully overlap the strips of leeks covering the interior of the mould. Carefully fill with the scallop mousse and cover again with the leeks and clingfilm. Place in a roasting tin half filled with water i.e. a bain-marie and cook in a moderate oven until lightly set.

For the choron sauce, take 1 dessertspoon of shallot confit with the egg yolks and an equal volume of wine and whisk over a gentle heat until light and slightly thick. Gradually add some clarified butter – whisking continuously until the sauce is thick and emulsified – add the chopped tomatoes, chives and seasoning.

For the scallops, pre-heat a thick-bottomed non-stick pan. Brush with clarified butter. Turn the pinwheels of scallops into the pan with the paper uppermost. Sear over a strong heat until the visible butter on the paper begins to melt.

To serve, place a cordon/ribbon of the sauce on a large plate and set the Anna potatoes on top with golden side uppermost. Place 2 dessertspoons of shallot confit on each potato. Present the pinwheel of scallops on top with the golden brown/seared side uppermost.

Cut the scallop mousse into 4 angled slices and arrange onto the pinwheel. Decorate each with a sprig of thyme.

Poached fillet of roe deer with tomato and parsnip essence

serves 6

1 saddle roe deer, approximately 3kg

2 free range chicken suprêmes

500ml red wine

800g celeriac

300g potato

400g green Savoy cabbage

500g parsnip

200g leek

200g celery

300g shallots

200g tomatoes

300g field mushrooms

6 bay leaves

1 bunch chervil

5 cloves of garlic

200g tomato purée

10 juniper berries

200g unsalted butter

2 eggs

30ml vegetable oil

20ml double cream

30g arrowroot

1 tablespoon soy sauce

1 tablespoon balsamic vinegar

10 black peppercorns

salt and milled pepper

Remove and trim 6 cutlets from the saddle leaving just 1 long rib bone attached. Remove and trim 3 fillets of 200g each. Trim and finely dice the remaining meat. Reserve the bones. Marinade the meat with 3 crushed cloves of garlic, juniper berries, bay leaves, crushed peppercorns and chervil stalks.

Wash and peel all the vegetables. Dice the leeks, celery and shallots. Thinly slice some parsnips into long triangles and dice the remainder. Cut the celeriac into julienne strips. Remove the large leaves from the cabbage and remove the centre stalks. Blanch and refresh the tomatoes. Remove and reserve the skins. Finely chop the heads off the field mushrooms. Finely chop the remaining garlic. Reserve some sprigs of chervil for the garnish and chop the remainder.

Prepare the chicken mousseline by adding the double cream to the puréed chicken breast and season. Add 1 clove of chopped garlic and 3 tablespoons of chopped chervil.

Set the bones to brown in a hot oven. Sauté the chopped leeks, celery and half the shallots until brown. Deglaze with the marinade. Add the browned bones and cover with water and simmer. Remove any grease and scum during cooking.

Sauté half of the roe deer trimmings with chopped shallots, garlic and chopped mushrooms. Deglaze with a little stock and season.

Blanch and refresh the cabbage leaves. Set 6 drained leaves on a clean cloth and season. Spoon some of the deer and mushroom mixture onto each one. Using a clean cloth, shape into 6 balls. Place these into a buttered casserole and add a little of the stock, cover and place in a moderate oven to braise for 30-40 minutes.

Cook and purée the parsnips. Put the purée in a muslin cloth and allow to drain – retain the liquor. Cook and purée the potatoes. Mix with the raw celeriac and season. Add 2 egg yolks and season. Shape into 6 galettes and refrigerate.

Divide the chicken mousse into 3 parts. Spread the mousse on 3 sheets of clingfilm to a thickness of 5mm to 6mm. Place a fillet of roe deer on each and wrap. Ensure that the fillet is completely covered with the mousse. Wrap each fillet in a double thickness of aluminium foil and seal the ends by twisting. Refrigerate.

Strain the stock and reduce by half. Cool this liquor quickly. Mix the parsnip purée with the remaining chopped roe deer. Mix in the tomato purée and the 2 egg whites. Add this clarification to the cold bouillon, bring to the boil and allow to simmer for 15 minutes. Carefully strain the liquor through a muslin cloth, season with the soy sauce and a little balsamic vinegar.

Place the fillets of roe deer into boiling water and poach for 12 minutes. Allow to rest for 2 minutes.

Sauté the celeriac galettes in a little oil and butter until golden brown. Keep warm. Season and carefully grill the marinated cutlets – keep pink. Deep fry the triangles of parsnip and the tomato skins – drain and season.

To serve, unwrap each fillet and cut at an angle into 2 pieces. Take 6 hot, large round plates. Place a galette on each and a column of fillet on the galette. Place a drained stuffed cabbage ball on each plate. Present a cutlet upright against the other 2 preparations. Pour a little of the essence around the plate and decorate with the deep fried parsnips, tomato skins and freshly picked chervil. Serve immediately with the remaining essence separately.

Hazelnut parfait with iced cassata and raspberry sorbet

serves 4-6

for the hazelnut parfait

240g caster sugar

6 egg yolks

20ml double cream

2 leaves gelatine

30ml double cream

2 tablespoons hazelnut gianduja
(a commercial chocolate and praline
paste, available from good
delicatessen's and pastry suppliers)

for the cassata/ ice cream

200g caster sugar boiled to soft ball
(118°C)

100g egg white

200ml double cream, lightly whipped

pistachios, chopped

glacé cherries, roughly chopped

rum soaked golden sultanas

for the raspberry sorbet

30ml water

500g caster sugar

500g raspberry purée

juice of 1 lemon

for the japonaise biscuits

100g egg white

100g caster sugar

100g ground hazelnuts

25g cornflour

30g caster sugar

To make the hazelnut parfait, soak the gelatine in a little water. Boil the double cream and whisk onto the egg yolks and sugar. Place in a clean pan and cook over a gentle heat. Add the soaked gelatine and place the pan over iced water and cool. Beat the double cream and fold into the mixture with the gianduja.

For the cassata, stiffly beat the egg whites and pour onto the boiling sugar syrup. Continue beating until cool. Fold in the lightly beaten cream and the chopped nuts and fruits. Freeze overnight.

For the raspberry sorbet, bring the sugar and water to the boil and pour over the purée and lemon juice. Allow to cool and place in a sorbetiere to churn and freeze.

To make the biscuits, beat the egg whites with 100g sugar until stiff. Mix the hazelnuts, cornflour and remaining sugar into the meringue mixture. Pipe through a plain nozzle onto silicon paper and bake at 165°C/Gas Mark 2¹/2 for approximately 20 minutes until light brown. Remove the paper and cool on a cake rack. Sandwich the cold parfait mix between 2 layers of biscuits and freeze overnight.

To serve, place a portion of cassata onto cold plates. Lightly dust the parfait with icing sugar and roughly cut into squares. Sit next to the cassata. Garnish with a portion of sorbet (this could be set on ornate pulled sugar spoons). Garnish with small mint sprigs and a little raspberry coulis.

THE PEAT INN

David Wilson

Dressed local Anstruther crab with yoghurt and lime and herb vinaigrette

serves 4

400g white crab meat

2 heaped tablespoons natural Greek yoghurt

juice of half a lime

2 level tablespoons chopped fresh coriander leaves

2 large tomatoes

50 mixed salad leaves (we use rocket, red chard and baby spinach)

for herb vinaigrette

50g freshly picked flat parsley, coriander and chervil

50ml Virgin olive oil

1 tablespoon white wine vinegar

juice of approximately 1/3 lemon

salt and pepper to taste

for tomato vinaigrette

1 tomato

3 tablespoons vegetable oil

2 tablespoons white wine vinegar

season to taste

Remove the meat from the crab claws, making sure there are no traces of shell left. Spoon the yoghurt into the crabmeat, mix thoroughly, add limejuice and mix again. If not using immediately cover the bowl with cling film and refrigerate. Just before serving, stir in the freshly chopped coriander leaves.

For the herb vinaigrette, put all the ingredients into a blender, except for the salt and pepper and blend to a smooth 'sauce' consistency. Check seasoning and adjust to taste.

For the tomato vinaigrette, process all the ingredients in a liquidiser until smooth. Strain through a fine sieve into a small bowl. Refrigerate until ready to serve.

To make the garnish, thinly slice the tomatoes and place on a silpat or non-stick mat on a baking sheet. Place on the middle shelf of a pre-heated oven 110°C/Gas 1/4 for about 2 hours until dried. Remove and place on a wire rack until cool. Store in an airtight container if not using immediately.

To serve, put the washed leaves in the centre of the plates. Place a ring mould on top and fill about 1/3 with dressed crab then place a slice of tomato on top. Continue layering. Finish with a slice of dried tomato and remove the ring mould. Drizzle herb vinaigrette over the salad leaves and decorate with dots of tomato vinaigrette.

Medallions of venison saddle on a wild mushroom cake with truffle sauce

serves 4

720g boned and trimmed venison saddle

for the mushroom cake

250g wild mushrooms, thinly sliced

20g unsalted butter

150ml milk

1 egg yolk

1 level dessertspoon corn flour

1 clove garlic, crushed

salt, pepper and nutmeg

for the truffle sauce

400ml game stock

5g dried ceps

20g unsalted butter

2 level tablespoons double cream

1 dash truffle essence

salt and pepper to taste

Slice the venison across the saddle into approximately 60g medallions, allowing 3 per person. Heat a film of oil in a sauté pan and cook the medallions on one side for 1 minute to seal and texture the meat, then turn over and cook for a further 30 seconds. Place in a roasting tray and cook in a pre-heated oven 220°C/Gas Mark 8 for 3 to 4 minutes. They should be pink in the centre.

To make the mushroom cake, melt the butter in a sauté pan. Add the mushrooms, stir gently until they begin to sweat, then add the milk, followed by the garlic and the corn flour. Keep stirring until all the corn flour has been absorbed in the milk.

Remove from the heat, beat the egg yolk and stir into the mushroom mixture. Season to taste. Keep in a warm oven until required.

To make the truffle sauce, bring the game stock with dried ceps to the boil in a saucepan over a gentle heat. Simmer for about 30 minutes until reduced by half. Add the cream and whisk in the cold butter pieces until all is amalgamated. Add the truffle essence and pass the sauce through a fine sieve into another saucepan. Check seasoning and keep until required.

To serve, spoon 3 small amounts of mushroom cake onto warm serving plates strategically placed near to the edge. Place a medallion of venison on top of the cakes, then spoon the truffle sauce over each medallion.

In the centre of each plate, place seasonal vegetables and potato.

Caramelised banana on a banana cake with coconut ice cream, coconut and caramel sauce

serves 4

4 bananas

for the banana bread

10g plain flour

50g granulated sugar

100g melted butter

2 ripe bananas

1 level teaspoon baking powder

3 eggs

for the coconut biscuits

1$^1/_2$ egg whites

50g caster sugar

30g desiccated coconut

30g sifted plain flour

30g melted butter

for the coconut ice cream

2 egg yolks

100g caster sugar

150ml milk

150ml double cream

100ml coconut cream

$^1/_2$ teaspoon liquid glucose

or the caramel for the bananas

100g caster sugar

100ml water

50ml boiling water

for the coconut/caramel sauce

100g caster sugar

100ml water

150ml double cream

100ml coconut cream

for the banana tuille

1 egg white

1 medium banana

To make the banana bread, peel the bananas and roughly chop. Place in food processor and work to a smooth purée. Pour the mixture into a bowl, add the sugar and mix together. Add the melted butter. Crack the eggs into another bowl, lightly beat and add to the banana mixture. Add half of the flour and baking powder. Mix together for about 1 minute, then add the rest and mix well.

To cook, place baking rings (80mm diameter) on a non-stick baking sheet. Spoon the mixture into rings approximately 10mm deep. Bake in pre-heated oven 180oC/ Gas Mark 4 for about 20 minutes until slightly risen and golden brown. Turn onto a wire rack to cool.

To make the coconut biscuits, whisk the egg whites and sugar together into peaks. Fold in the sifted flour and coconut and add the melted butter. Spoon onto a silpat mat or non-stick mat on a baking sheet and spread into approximately

80mm diameter round shapes to make biscuits. Bake in a pre-heated oven 210°C/Gas Mark 7 until light golden. Remove with a spatula and place on a wire rack to cool. If not using immediately store in an airtight container.

To make the ice cream, bring the milk and cream to the boil and add the liquid glucose. In a Pyrex bowl, whisk the egg yolks and sugar together until pale in colour. Slowly add the boiled milk and cream into the egg mixture and whisk together. Place over a pan of water on a gentle heat and stir constantly until it coats the back of a spoon. Remove the bowl from the saucepan and place in a large bowl with cold water and ice. When cool add the coconut cream.

To make the caramel for the bananas, place the sugar and water in a heavy bottomed pan. Bring to the boil to make golden caramel. Add the boiling water and stir together. Keep to one side until required.

To make the coconut/caramel sauce, put the sugar and water in a pan and bring to the boil to caramelise. The colour should be golden tan. Add the cream and coconut cream stirring together over the heat for about 2 minutes. Keep to one side until required.

To make the tuille, purée the banana and egg white together until smooth. Spread onto a silpat mat or a non-stick mat on an oven sheet in a very thin layer. Bake in pre-heated oven at 110°C/Gas Mark 1/4 for about 45 minutes or until set enough to cut. Cut into strips about 25mm wide x 100mm long. Lift strips from the baking sheet to loosen and return to the oven. Continue baking a further 10/15 minutes until strong enough to shape. Twist to desired shape. Store in airtight container until required.

To cook the bananas, peel and slice them into pieces about 15mm thick. Pour some caramel into a large sauté pan over a gentle heat. Place the banana pieces into the caramel and cook for 2/3 minutes until one side of the bananas is caramelised, then turn over and caramelise the other side. Keep warm.

To serve, warm the banana bread and place in the centre of the serving plates. Place approximately 6 slices of caramelised banana on top, then a coconut biscuit on top of that. Put 3 banana pieces at the top and bottom of each plate. Run coconut/caramel sauce around the edge. Place a ball of coconut ice cream on top of the biscuit and decorate with banana tuille. Serve immediately.

NEW HALL

Simon Malin

Grilled scallops with cauliflower cream and caviar

serves 4

*12 large scallops
(preferably hand-dived,
available from good fishmongers)*

1 cauliflower

100ml double cream

a few drops of truffle oil

salt

sugar

half a lemon

1 punnet of lambs lettuce

1 tomato

25g Oscietra caviar

Firstly open the scallops and remove everything apart from the white meat. Wash under cold water to rinse away any dirt, pat dry on kitchen paper and leave to firm up in the fridge for 1 hour.

Cut the cauliflower into florets and boil in salted water until tender, drain. Bring the cream to the boil and liquidise with the cauliflower until smooth. Season and keep warm.

Peel and chop the tomato into even squares. Wash the lettuce.

Cut each scallop into 3 depending on size and rub the slices with a little olive oil. Sauté quickly until golden brown for between 30 seconds and 1 minute. Turn over, season with salt, sugar and a squeeze of lemon.

To serve, spoon a small amount of the cauliflower cream into the centre of a plate, lay the scallop slices on top, dress the lambs lettuce with a little truffle oil and assemble on the top. Garnish with the tomato and a nice spoon of caviar.

Fillet of Scotch beef with Parma ham and wild mushrooms

serves 4

4 x 225g tournedos

4 slices Parma ham

250g spinach

2 large Besinée potatoes

2 shallots

100ml Madeira jus or sauce

selection of wild mushrooms

100g garlic butter

100ml clarified butter

2 large parsnips

100ml double cream

salt and pepper

Very lightly season each fillet of beef and wrap in a slice of Parma ham.

Peel and chop the parsnip, boil in lightly salted water until tender and drain. Bring the cream to the boil and blend with the parsnip until smooth. Keep warm.

Peel the potatoes and grate. Fry in small batches in the clarified butter until golden brown. Slice the shallots finely and fry in the remaining fat from the potatoes until crisp.

Next, in a pan, seal the beef on all sides and transfer to a roasting tray. Roast in a hot oven 200°C/Gas Mark 6 for about 7 minutes. Leave to rest for 10 minutes.

To serve, sauté the wild mushrooms in the garlic butter and season. Cook the spinach in a little of the garlic butter for about 30 seconds to a minute until tender; season and drain. Place the spinach in the centre of each plate, followed by the potato and beef. Spoon a small amount of the parsnip purée on top and sprinkle with fried shallots. Arrange the wild mushrooms around the outside and drizzle Madeira jus to suit.

Whole roast peach with honey and lavender ice cream

serves 4

4 large peaches
100g softened butter
100g honey

for the ice cream

500ml milk
500ml double cream
12 egg yolks
50g sugar
200g honey
4 sprigs of lavender

First make the ice cream. Bring the cream to the boil with the lavender and leave to infuse for 20 minutes. Whisk the eggs, sugar and honey together. Pour in the cream and stir all the time. Return to the heat and stir until custard coats the back of a spoon but do not allow to boil. Pass through a fine sieve and leave to cool. Then churn in an ice cream machine.

Mix the honey and butter together. Blanch the peaches, peel and pat dry. Make a cross in the top of each one. Brush with the butter mix, place on a roasting tray and bake in a hot oven 200°C/Gas Mark 6 for 12 minutes.

Serve with a ball of the ice cream and a few berries to garnish.

PORTMARNOCK HOTEL & GOLF LINKS

Stefan Matz

Fresh herb crusted fillet of turbot on a black and white seafood pudding

serves 8

8 turbot fillets, 80g each

3 slices of white bread, decrusted

1 small bunch of flat parsley and tarragon

for the puddings

400g turbot fillet, skinless

3 scallops, finely diced

50g smoked salmon

100g crab meat

300g cream

1 sachet of squid ink

salt and pepper

for the garnish

16 baby carrots, peeled and blanched

16 green asparagus tips, blanched

16 scallions, blanched
(scallions - immature onions)

1 small head of curly endive lettuce, washed

100g extra virgin olive oil

30g balsamic vinegar

To make the puddings, slice the quantity of turbot required for the pudding finely, chill well and place in a food processor. Season with salt and pepper and combine with the cream by adding it slowly to the fish and mixing it in the processor to produce a smooth mousse. Reserving one half of the mousse for the white seafood pudding, the squid ink and smoked salmon is added to the other half of mousse in the processor and mixed well until completely black, then fold in the diced scallops. Fold in the crabmeat to the reserved half of the mousse to finish the white pudding. Adjust the seasoning of both puddings.

Spread both mousses separately on parchment paper and roll into a sausage shape. Tie both puddings with string and poach at 85°C for approximately 45 minutes until fully cooked. Chill and slice to the desired thickness.

To make the breadcrumbs, pick 8 nice sprigs of tarragon and chervil each and reserve for garnish. Mix the remaining herb leaves with the bread to make fine green coloured breadcrumbs.

Season the turbot fillets with salt and pepper and cook together with 8 black and white seafood pudding slices each, in a very hot griddle pan, turning the fish and the pudding after a few minutes. Layer the turbot fillets evenly with the breadcrumbs and finish in a preheated oven 180°C/Gas Mark 4, for another few minutes only. While cooking the fish, warm the vegetables gently in the olive oil using a sauce pan, season to taste

To serve, arrange the vegetables on the plates, place the endive lettuce in the centre and layer with the fish fillets and pudding slices. Stir the vinegar gently into the warm olive oil and drizzle onto the plate garnishing with the herb sprigs. Serve hot.

Roast saddle of mountain lamb, flavoured with roast garlic and fine herbs with mildly spiced carrot sauce

serves 8

1kg fully trimmed and skinned loin of Mountain lamb, cut into 2 parts of equal length

1 French trimmed rack of lamb - 8 bones

2 fully trimmed lamb fillets

*100g crepinette of pork
(sausage lining - available from the butcher), washed*

for the lamb mousse

250g finely minced lean lamb from the leg

250g cream

egg yolk

100g white breadcrumbs

*assorted fresh herbs -
basil, tarragon, rosemary, thyme, flat parsley, washed and chopped*

*2 cloves of garlic,
slowly roasted in the oven*

salt and pepper

for the sauce

200g carrot juice

200g white wine

200g white chicken or vegetable stock

juice of 1/2 lemon

cajun spices

60g butter

salt

for the garnish

8 portions of French beans, blanched and split

2 tomatoes, skinned and diced

8 sprigs of rosemary

16 roasted potatoes

grated nutmeg

To make the herb and garlic mousse, place the minced lamb, herbs, egg yolk and garlic in a food processor and season well. Blend by adding the cream slowly until the mousse is smooth and green, then fold in the breadcrumbs.

Place the crepinette on a cloth and spread with some of the mousse. Place the two loins on top side by side and cover with some mousse. The two fillets are set side by side on top of the loins and covered with the remaining mousse. Roll the crepinette tightly round the mousse and meat to give it the shape of a lamb saddle and tie with string.

Season the rack of lamb and seal it with the saddle in a large frying pan on all sides and place in a preheated oven 180°C/Gas Mark 4,

cooking it to your liking (approximately 10 minutes for the rack and 25 to 35 minutes for the saddle). After cooking allow the saddle to rest for at least 5 minutes.

While cooking the meat reduce the carrot juice with the stock, lemon juice and white wine to 1/3 of the original amount, season with salt and spices and fold in the butter to thicken the sauce, keep hot.

To serve, sauté the beans in a little butter, add the tomatoes and season with salt, pepper and nutmeg, place in the centre of the plates. Carve the saddle and rack into eight slices and set on top of the beans. Place the roasted potatoes and pour the carrot sauce around the meat and potatoes, garnishing with sprigs of rosemary.

Strawberry and rhubarb crumble

Strawberry and rhubarb crumble

serves 8

8 puff pastry discs, 4" in diameter

1 bunch of rhubarb, peeled

3 punnets of strawberries

75g caster sugar

for the crumble mix

120g plain flour

50g soft butter

50g brown sugar

for the tuille pastry

1 egg white

25g icing sugar

30g soft butter

25g soft flour

10g cocoa powder

for the garnish

8 mint sprigs

100g natural yoghurt

vanilla flavoured ice cream

strawberry sorbet

icing sugar

Slice half of the rhubarb into small sticks 2-2^1/$_2$" long, chop the remaining rhubarb and place in saucepan, sprinkle with the sugar and allow to stand for 30 minutes. Slice one half of the strawberries and add the remainder to the chopped rhubarb and cook gently until very soft, liquidize and chill.

For the crumble mix simply combine all ingredients to form crumbs. Then make the tuille pastry by mixing all ingredients to a smooth paste and place in a piping bag with a very fine nozzle. Pipe into desired shapes and bake at 180°C/Gas Mark 4 until crisp.

Spread the rhubarb and strawberry sauce (reserving a small quantity for garnish) onto the puff pastry discs and layer with rhubarb sticks and strawberry slices, top generously with the crumble mix. Bake the crumbles in a preheated oven at 200°C/Gas Mark 6, for approximately 12 minutes, dust with icing sugar and keep hot.

To serve, place dots of strawberry and rhubarb sauce and natural yoghurt on the plate, set the crumble in the centre and top with one scoop each of ice cream and sorbet, garnish with baked spirals of tuille pastry and mint sprigs.

BINDON COUNTRY HOUSE HOTEL

Patrick Robert

Seared scallops on broccoli purée with orange pomme fondant and smoked dressing

serves 4

16 scallops

4 large potatoes

1 orange

olive oil

juice of 1 lemon

1 sprig of thyme

1 bay leaf

1 clove of garlic

300g butter

2 large heads of broccoli

for the dressing

2 chopped shallots

1 large tomato

4 chives

50ml raspberry vinegar

150ml smoke oil

10 black olives

Cook the broccoli in salted, boiling water until soft. Drain and place in a food processor with 80g of the butter and some black pepper. Blend to a very thin purée and keep warm. Heat 200g of butter in a pan. Add the orange zest, thyme, garlic and bay leaf. Using a 5cm round cutter, cut the potatoes, place in the pan and cook until soft. Season the scallops and cook them briefly in a very hot pan in a little olive oil, turning when well caramelised. Stir in the remaining 20g of butter and add the lemon juice.

To serve, put 4 spoonfuls of the broccoli puree around the edge of each serving plate and place a scallop on the top of each one. Place a potato in the middle and the dressing on the top of it and in between the scallops.

Pan-fried fillet of beef with wild mushrooms, foie gras and truffle sauce

serves 4

4 beef fillets

4 slices of foie gras

200g spinach

12 minted potatoes, boiled and peeled

2 cloves of garlic

4 handfuls of wild mushrooms

1 truffle

2 dessertspoons of chopped fresh chives

salt and pepper to taste

4 sprigs of fresh thyme

for the truffle sauce

1/2 litre chicken stock

1 teaspoon white truffle paste

1 grated black truffle

salt and pepper

Using a 4 x 4cm diameter galette mould, combing the thyme, salt and pepper with boiled potatoes pressing down to fill all the gaps. Using a spatula, even the potatoes so that they are flushed with the tops of the moulds. Place the moulds in the oven 200°C/Gas Mark 6 for about 8 minutes. Heat 10g butter in a pan, add the spinach and some seasoning. Cook until wilted and drain on kitchen paper.

For the truffle sauce, reduce the stock to 50ml, remove from the heat and add the truffles, salt and pepper.

Trim, clean and wash the mushrooms and drain on kitchen paper. Cook them in a little oil and season. Add chives and crushed garlic.

Season the foie gras and heat the frying pan. When it is hot, cook for 2 minutes on each side.

Season the beef with salt and pepper. Heat the oil and butter in a frying pan. When it has melted, sear on both sides. Cook in the oven at 190°C/Gas Mark 5 for 4 minutes each side. Remove from the oven and allow to rest for 10 minutes.

To serve, place the spinach and the potatoes in the centre of the plate. Put the seared beef on one side, the mushrooms and foie gras on the other side and pour the truffle sauce all around the plate.

151

Selection of sorbets served with poached peach, clotted cream and lavender and black pepper syrup

serves 4

1 litre of peach coulis

1 litre of mango coulis

1 litre blackcurrant coulis

for the stock syrup

1.5kg caster sugar

1$^1/_2$ litres of water

3 teaspoons of glucose syrup

Dissolve the sugar in the water in a heavy-based saucepan over a low heat and bring to the boil. Cool, then mix in the glucose syrup. Mix 1 litre of the stock syrup with 1 litre of peach coulis and do the same with the other 2. Churn in an ice-cream machine until almost solid. Transfer to a suitable container to store in the freezer.

for the poached peach

2 peaches

250ml stock syrup - 150ml water and 100g caster sugar

Make the stock syrup as before. Leave to cool. Put the peaches in a saucepan and pour over the cold syrup to cover. Bring to the boil, then refresh straight away in iced water. Peel before completely cold. Keep the stock syrup and add 1 handful of black peppercorns and 1 handful of fresh lavender.

for the tuile baskets

3 egg whites

140g icing sugar

110g flour

425g liquid butter

Whisk the egg whites, then add sugar, flour and butter. Place a round mould, 6cm diameter on a baking sheet and fill with the mixture. Level off to the same thickness as the mould and cook in the oven 200°C/Gas Mark 6. Once golden brown, place the tuile disc on top of a metal fluted tartlet mould and place a second one on the top. Press to form the shape.

To serve, place half of a peach in the middle of a plate. Scoop a little clotted cream with a warm teaspoon and put on the top of the peach with a sprig of fresh mint. Pass the syrup through a sieve and pour over the top of the peach. Arrange the little tuile baskets on the plate with a small amount of melted chocolate underneath to prevent them moving and scoop the sorbets into them.

153

Neville Campbell

Tortellini Landes foie gras

serves 4

100g foie gras trimmings

25g shallots, chopped

25g wild mushrooms, chopped

1 small truffle, finely diced

1 packet of wonton wrappers

1 egg, beaten

4 slices of raw foie gras

salt and freshly ground black pepper

For the prune jus

500ml veal stock or good-quality beef stock

250g prunes, plus 8 for garnish

1 glass of red wine

For the beurre blanc

1 glass of white wine

3 large shallots, finely chopped

a few sprigs of thyme

200g chilled unsalted butter, cut into small cubes, plus extra for frying the mushrooms

75g wild mushrooms

chopped fresh chives

To make the tortellini, mix together the foie gras trimmings, shallots, wild mushrooms and truffle and season with salt and pepper. Brush the wonton wrappers with beaten egg (this will seal the filling in), then place a small amount of the filling in the centre of each one. Fold the wrapper into a semi-circle, pull in the tips until both ends meet and then press them together. Chill until needed

To make the prune jus, put the stock, prunes and red wine in a pan and simmer until reduced to a fairly syrupy consistency. Pass through a fine sieve, pushing with the back of a ladle so some of the prune pulp goes through, and then set aside.

To make the beurre blanc, put the wine, shallots and thyme into a pan and simmer until the wine has reduced to a glaze. Whisk in the butter a few pieces at a time until it emulsifies and then strain the sauce into a clean pan. Season to taste.

Cook the tortellini in lightly salted boiling water, then drain well. In a little butter, quickly sauté the wild mushrooms for the beurre blanc until tender, seasoning with salt and pepper. In a separate pan, sauté the foie gras for 30 seconds on each side. Heat the prunes and keep warm.

Place the foie gras slices in the centre of each serving plate, place the prunes on top and then arrange the tortellini around the foie gras. Coat the tortellini with the prune jus. Add the sautéed mushrooms to the beurre blanc and bring to the boil carefully. Add the chives and spoon the sauce over the tortellini.

Baked sea bass with crispy fennel skin

serves 4

1 large shallot, chopped

a pinch of saffron

175ml white wine

250ml fish stock

100ml double cream

4 x 175g sea bass fillets

oil for deep-frying

25g fennel seeds, crushed

5g rock salt

a pinch of yukari seasoning (available from Japanese shops)

a pinch of cayenne pepper

olive oil

For the braised fennel

1 fennel bulb, cut into batons 4mm thick

chicken stock

a knob of butter

salt and freshly ground black pepper

Put the shallot, saffron, white wine and fish stock in a pan and boil until reduced by half, then add the cream and reduce by half again. Set aside.

For the braised fennel, put the fennel into a pan, half cover with stock, then add the butter and some salt and pepper. Cover and braise until tender.

To make the crispy fennel skin, skin the sea bass fillets and set the fillets aside. Remove the scales from the skin, blanch it in a pan of boiling water for 2 seconds, then plunge it into ice-cold water. Drain well. Pat the skin dry with a cloth, cut it into rectangles and deep-fry in hot oil until crisp. Drain well and flatten gently to obtain a perfect shape; trim with scissors. Coat with the crushed fennel seeds and rock salt and then garnish with diagonal strips of yukari seasoning and cayenne pepper.

Sauté the fish briefly in a little olive oil until golden brown on both sides, then transfer it to an oven preheated to 220°C/Gas Mark 7 to finish cooking. Meanwhile, reheat the sauce and the braised fennel.

To serve, place the braised fennel on each plate, put the fish on top and then put the crispy skin on top of the fish. Pour the sauce around the plate.

Pandan pudding with blueberry compôte

serves 4

*40g fresh pandan leaves
(available from Thai and Malaysian
shops), chopped*

200ml skimmed milk

200ml double cream

zest of 1 orange

zest of 1 lemon

1 vanilla pod

6 eggs, separated

100g caster sugar

2 gelatine leaves

For the blueberry compôte

350g blueberries

50g caster sugar

$^1/_4$ cinnamon stick

$^1/_4$ fresh red chilli

Liquidise the pandan leaves and milk until they become a rich green colour. Put the mixture into a pan with the cream and the orange and lemon zest. Split the vanilla pod open and scrape out the seeds, then add the pod and seeds to the pan and bring to the boil. Meanwhile, mix together the egg yolks and half the sugar in a bowl. Pour the pandan mixture on to the yolks, stirring all the time, then return to the pan and cook, stirring constantly, until the mixture has thickened enough to coat the back of the spoon. Remove from the heat. Soak the gelatine leaves in cold water for 5 minutes, then drain well and stir into the custard until dissolved. Pass the mixture through a fine sieve and cool rapidly.

Whisk the egg whites to soft peaks and fold in the remaining sugar. Fold the egg whites into the custard when it is nearly cold, then spoon the mixture into 4 square lined moulds and leave in the fridge to set.

Meanwhile, make the blueberry compôte. Heat 250g of the blueberries in a pan with the sugar and a dash of water until the sugar has dissolved, then blitz to a purée in a blender. Add the cinnamon, chilli and remaining blueberries and leave to cool.

To serve, turn out the puddings on to 4 plates. Hollow out a square hole about 5mm deep in each one. Arrange the blueberries from the compote in lines in the holes, then pour in enough of the liquid so that the blueberries are almost covered. Serve with the remaining compôte.

NEWICK PARK

Billy Butcher

12 hand-dived scallops

for the herb oil

4 bunches basil

2 bunches flat leaf parsley

1 bunch dill

200ml olive oil

for the risotto

2 banana shallots

50g butter

300g Arborio risotto rice

100g grated Parmesan

1 litre vegetable stock

for the croûtes

12 slices of baguette

drizzle of olive oil

1 clove garlic

for the rouille

1 red pepper

2 cloves garlic

1 slice of white bread

1 egg yolk

1 teaspoon Dijon mustard

125ml olive oil

for the bouillabaisse

1 head fennel

2 carrots

1 leek

^{1}/$_2$ onion

^{1}/$_4$ head celery

2 pinches saffron powder

5 tomatoes

2 star anise

6 cardamoms

2 tablespoon tomato purée

^{1}/$_2$ litre white wine

^{1}/$_2$ litre orange juice

^{1}/$_2$ litre water

675g fish on the bone

12 sprigs chervil

To make the herb oil, pick all the herbs and blanch for 1 minute in boiling water. Strain and refresh in cold water. Squeeze all the excess water from the herbs and blend in a food processor with the olive oil for 2-5 minutes. Hang in muslin or butter cloth for 2 hours in the fridge (to keep its vibrant colour). Retain the green oil for garnish later and set the green pulp aside.

To make the croûtes, place the baguette slices on an oven tray and drizzle oil over them and season. Place in moderate oven for 5 minutes until golden brown. Leave to cool down and rub with garlic and set aside.

For the rouille, roast the pepper in the oven until the skin is charred. Take out, remove the skin and leave to cool. Put all the ingredients, except for the oil, into a blender. Finely purée and slowly add the oil. Remove from the blender and season.

Roast all the ingredients for the bouillabaisse in a hot oven until golden brown. Place in saucepan with all the liquids and simmer for 40 minutes. Blend the sauce like a soup and push through a metal sieve with a ladle. Put back on the stove and reduce by two thirds.

Pan fried diver scallops with herb risotto, garlic croûtes, bouillabaisse juices and rouille

serves 4

To make the risotto, melt the butter in a thick-bottomed pan and sweat the finely diced shallots without colour. Then add the rice and carry on sweating for a further 5 minutes. Slowly add the hot stock and keep stirring until all the liquid has been absorbed. Remove from the heat and add the Parmesan, crème fraîche, herb pulp and seasoning.

To serve, take 3 metal rings, 5cm in diameter and 2cm high and place to one side of the bowl. In the top ring, completely fill with risotto, next ring down - only fill half way and the bottom ring - only line the base. Remove the rings and flood each bowl with bouillabaisse. On top of the risotto, place a croûte.

Fry the seasoned scallops in a pan with a little olive oil. Now place one scallop on each of the croûtes with a quenelle of rouille on top and garnish with a sprig of chervil. With the green oil that was kept from making the pulp, arrange 5 puddles on the other side of the plate.

Roast loin of lamb with mutabal, braised baby fennel and chorizo sausage

serves 4

1 loin of lamb cut into 4 canons
ie 4 portions

4 chorizo sausages

100g butter

for the mutabal

4 aubergines

30g crème fraîche

1 bunch chopped chives

juice of half a lemon

for the baby fennel

12 baby fennel

1 litre orange juice

1 litre white wine

6 star anise

3 cloves garlic

4 sprigs of thyme

for the basil oil

2 bunches basil

100ml olive oil

for the chorizo oil

2 chorizo sausages

100ml olive oil

1 teaspoon paprika

for the crisps

12 thin slices aubergine

12 thin slices beef steak tomatoes

12 leaves of basil

For the baby fennel, start by cutting

the tops off just above the main bulb. Place in a stainless steel pan and add all the ingredients. Cover with greaseproof paper and cook at 170°C/Gas Mark 3 for 1 hour. Check that the fennel is soft before removing from the oven and set aside in cooking juices.

To make the middle eastern mutabal, place the aubergines under the grill on a high heat turning regularly, they will take about 45 minutes to 1 hour. Do not be afraid to burn them, as this will add to the char grill flavour. When done, remove and allow to cool. Split in half lengthways and remove the flesh. Place in a butter cloth or muslin and squeeze out the excess liquid. Then place in a bowl, add the rest of the ingredients, mix well, season and place in a saucepan ready to be warmed up.

For the basil oil, pick the basil and blanch in boiling water for 1 minute. Refresh in cold water and squeeze out excess water. Put in a blender with the oil and blend for 5 minutes and pass through a sieve. Keep for later.

For the chorizo oil, finely chop up the sausage and gently fry in the olive oil. Add the paprika and continue cooking gently until deep red in colour. Pass through a sieve and leave until required.

To make the crisps, place the tomato slices on a non-stick tray with a drizzle of olive oil and seasoning and bake in a low oven for 2 hours until they have crisped up. Deep fry the aubergines and basil leaves on a low heat so they don't burn. Once crisp, soak up the excess oil on kitchen paper.

For the canons of lamb, ask your butcher to clean them up and to remove any sinew. Season and sear in a frying pan with olive oil to seal. Add 100g of butter and keep moving the pan on the stove until the butter turns frothy. Then add the chorizo sausages and gently colour them. You'll find that the natural oils will come out of the sausages and flavor the lamb. Cook for 5 minutes and rest for a further 5 minutes to achieve nice pink pieces of lamb.

To serve, put 3 quenelles of the mutabal at the top of the plate. Cut the chorizo into 3 at an angle and stand them up in a back to front C shape at the bottom of the plate. Lay the 3 baby fennel against them. On top of the mutabal place the lamb, cut the same way as the sausage with the cut side of the meat facing out towards you. On top of the lamb, place an aubergine crisp on each, followed by the tomato crisp and finely the basil leaves. Drizzle the oils all around the plate.

Iced honey and poppy seed parfait with chocolate sorbet and caramelised strawberries

serves 4

for the parfait

5 egg yolks

145g caster sugar

270ml cream

50ml water

50ml honey

50g poppy seeds

for the sorbet

100ml milk

100ml water

60g caster sugar

20g glucose

80g dark chocolate

for the chocolate sauce

160ml whipping cream

25g cocoa powder

75g caster sugar

80ml water

for the caramel

150g glucose

100g fondant patissier

for the strawberry coulis

300ml strawberry purée

150ml stock syrup

20 strawberries

4 sprigs of Mint

icing sugar

filo pastry

egg wash

To make the parfait, semi-whip the cream and put in the fridge. Cream the yolks. Boil the sugar and water to 120°C and pour onto the creamed yolk mixture. Carry on mixing until cold, then fold in the cream, and add the honey and poppy seeds. Pour mixture into 4 metal rings, 7cm in diameter and 4cm high and set in the freezer for 8 hours.

For the sorbet, bring all the ingredients to the boil except for the chocolate. Take off the heat, whisk in the chocolate and bring back to the boil. Pass through a sieve, cool down and chill. Churn in ice-cream machine and set in the freezer for 4 hours.

To make the chocolate sauce, bring all the ingredients to boil and whisk well, take off the heat, pass through a sieve and place in the fridge.

For the strawberry coulis, boil both the puree and syrup together and pass through a sieve. Set aside for later.

Unroll the filo pastry sheets and cut 24 discs, 9cm in diameter. Butter and sprinkle each disc with icing sugar and layer them up 3 high, so you should have 8 piles of 3. Place on a non-stick tray and bake in a moderate oven until golden brown. Remove from the oven and leave to cool down.

For the caramel, place the glucose and fondant patissier in a thick bottomed pan and slowly bring up to 160°c. Take off the heat and cool down so the caramel thickens up. With a cocktail stick, put it through the bottom of the strawberry and dip the point of the strawberry in the caramel and skewer in the side of a cardboard box. Gravity will pull the sugar off the strawberry to produce a strawberry with a caramel spike. When all the strawberries are done, remove from the box and stand so the point is facing upright. Then remove the cocktail sticks.

To make sugar cages with the remaining caramel, take a greased ladle and fork and dip the fork into the caramel and dribble around the base on the outside of the ladle, then repeat crossing the lines to make a cage.

To serve, place a filo disc in the center of the plate. Remove the rings from the parfaits by warming with the palm of _____ ce on the filo discs and top with another disc. Place 1 ball of the chocolate sorbet on top and cover with a sugar cage. Put 5 puddles of chocolate sauce around the parfait and within those puddles put 5 puddles of strawberry sauce. Then in between the sauces, put 5 caramelized strawberries. Garnish with a sprig of mint on the top filo sheet and dust with icing sugar.

Chef's tips – make the caramel strawberries as late as possible so they keep their crunch and don't start dissolving.

When making the sugar cages, if the sugar goes cold put back on heat and warm up and just start again, this is the reason for using glucose and fondant patissier rather than sugar and water.

THE DEVONSHIRE ARMS

Steve Williams

Jerusalem artichoke mousse with herb purée and langoustines

serves 4

For the jelly

200ml lemon juice

4 tablespoons glucose syrup

freshly picked thyme leaves

1/2 leaf gelatine, soaked in cold water

For the mousse

50g butter

400g Jerusalem artichokes, peeled and sliced

200ml single cream

salt and pepper

2 leaves gelatine, soaked in cold water

For the herb purée

50g parsley

50g basil

50g chives

100g spinach

2 dessertspoons glucose syrup

For the jelly, bring the lemon juice and glucose to boiling point and add the thyme and gelatine. Slightly chill and pour into moulds and leave to set.

Lightly sweat the artichokes in butter, add the cream and cook gently until soft. Liquidize the artichokes and pass through a fine sieve. Add the gelatine and season to taste. Pour into the moulds.

For the herb purée, blanch all the herbs and squeeze dry. Add the glucose, liquidize until smooth and pass through a fine sieve.

To serve, de-mould the mousse. Pan-fry the langoustines. Place the puree in the centre of a bowl and place the mousse on top. Arrange the langoustines around the edge and garnish with deep-fried globe artichokes and freshly picked thyme.

NB: a little vinaigrette of shellfish could enhance the dish.

Medallions of veal with braised celery hearts and Scottish girolles

serves 2

2 x 170g veal fillets

2-3 large Maris Piper potatoes

clarified butter

100g spinach, picked and washed

12 girolle mushrooms, cleaned and washed

20g rosemary, chopped

2 hearts of celery

1 litre chicken stock

250ml beef glace (reduced beef stock)

100ml olive oil

Wash and peel the potatoes. Using a suitable sized mould, cut out a barrel shape from the potatoes that is the same size as the moulds to be used for the cooking. Slice the potatoes approximately 2mm thick and blanch in a pan of boiling water for just a few seconds. Take out and place onto a cloth. Pat dry and season.

Warm the clarified butter and grease the moulds. Layer by layer place the potatoes in the mould adding a little chopped rosemary and clarified butter between each slice of potato until approximately 1cm above the height of the mould. Roast in a bath of very hot oil and cook until both crisp and soft. Reserve

Trim down the celery by removing the tops and peel the remainder of the heart. Carefully trim the root. Place into the lightly seasoned chicken stock with rosemary, bay leaf, peppercorns and a clove of garlic. Cover with a cartouche (a piece of greased paper tied over the dish with a hole in the middle) and braise until tender.

To make the sauce, pass the celery braising liquor through a fine sieve and reduce by half. Add the beef glace, a tablespoon of cream and olive oil. Liquidize and pass again through a fine sieve. Finish with chopped rosemary and a squeeze of lemon. Reserve.

To serve, season and pan fry the veal fillets in foaming butter until pink. Turn out the potatoes from their moulds. Cook the remaining vegetables and arrange on the plates with the veal, celery and potato.

A little rosemary oil can help flavour and presentation.

Minted marquise of chocolate and cappuccino ice cream

serves 4

For the preparation of chocolate/marquise

165g soft butter

150g cocoa powder

280ml double cream

70g icing sugar

150g bitter chocolate

4 egg yolks

150g caster sugar

For the chocolate sauce

125g cocoa

150ml water

185g sugar

30g chopped mint

For the ice cream

290ml cream

290ml milk

6 egg yolks

115g sugar

3 tablespoons ground Expresso beans

1 tablespoon coffee essence

For the marquise, melt the butter and cocoa in a bowl over a pan of water on a gentle heat i.e. a bain marie. Whisk the cream and icing sugar to ribbon stage. Melt the chocolate in a bain marie. Whisk the sugar and yolks until thick. Fold in the chocolate and the butter and mix in the cream. Pipe into timbale moulds leaving a hole in the centre and reserve

For the chocolate sauce, bring all the ingredients to the boil together in a pan and cool. Pour into the centre of the timbale mould and seal with more marquise mix.

For the ice cream, bring the milk and cream to boiling point and add the mixed sugar and yolks. Add to that the expresso beans and coffee essence. Cool and churn in an ice cream maker.

To serve, place a serving of ice cream on the plates with some marquise filled with the chocolate sauce.

AMBERLEY CASTLE

James Peyton

Millefeuille of caramelised foie gras, apple and parsnip with confit shallots and Madeira sauce

serves 4

8 slices of foie gras

4 slices of apple, peeled and cored, 8mm thick and 6cm round

4 slices of potato, peeled and blanched, 8mm thick and 6cm round

4 slices of parsnip, peeled and blanched 8mm thick and 6cm round

12 small peeled shallots

250g spinach

300ml goose fat

50g sugar

25g butter

salt and pepper

chervil for garnish

oil and butter for cooking

for the sauce

500ml veal stock, or a rich beef stock available from good supermarkets

400ml Madeira

12 button mushrooms, sliced

6 shallots, sliced

2 sprigs of thyme

2 sprigs of rosemary

1 clove of garlic, chopped

35g butter

salt and pepper

To make the sauce, brown the shallots, mushrooms and garlic in a saucepan, then add the Madeira and reduce to a syrup. Add the stock and simmer until it has a thick, coating consistency, skimming constantly during this process. Then remove the pan from the heat and season with salt and pepper, infuse thyme and rosemary, then pass the mixture through double muslin into another pan and reserve until ready to complete the dish.

For the millefeuille, warm the goose fat, add the shallots and keep on a low heat until they are soft and translucent. When all mis en place is prepared and you are ready to serve, sauté the potato in a little oil and butter until golden brown. In a separate pan, melt the 25g of butter over a medium heat, add the parsnip and apple. Sauté until golden brown before adding the sugar. Remove from the pan and keep hot.

Sauté the spinach with a little oil, salt and pepper until just soft and place on a cloth to soak up the excess liquid. Finally, bring your sauce to the boil and whisk the 35g of butter in at the last minute. Sear the slices of foie gras in a red-hot pan and season with salt and pepper.

To serve, place the spinach in the centre of 4 plates and layer with potato, then foie gras, apple, foie gras again and parsnip on top. Arrange the shallots at 3 points on the plate. Pour the sauce around and garnish with chervil.

Fillet of John Dory with stuffed piquillos peppers, chargrilled Mediterranean vegetables, wild rocket and light lime vierge

serves 4

4 x 300g John Dory fillets

500g wild rocket

salt and pepper

oil and butter for cooking

for the stuffed peppers

12 piquillos peppers

12 chargrilled artichokes, chopped

100g sun blushed tomatoes, chopped

1 shallot, chopped

2 cloves of garlic, chopped

25ml olive oil

salt and pepper

for the chargrilled vegetables

3 courgettes, sliced lengthways, 5mm thick

1 aubergine, skinned, 10mm thick and cut into diamonds

for the lime vierge

12 limes or 100ml lime juice and zest

100ml olive oil

3 tomatoes, skinned, deseeded and chopped into dice

a handful of chopped basil

salt and pepper

Sear the piquillos peppers on the char grill, then sweat the garlic and shallot in 25ml of olive oil and combine with the artichokes and sun blushed tomatoes. Take the mixture and stuff the peppers, then reserve wrapped in buttered papers, until you are ready to heat and serve.

For the vierge, take the juice and the zest of the limes (100ml in total) and add 100ml of olive oil. Add salt and pepper to taste, then liquidise until a thick dressing forms. Add the basil and tomatoes just before serving.

Take 12 strips of courgette and 12 diamonds of aubergine, rub with a little olive oil, season and char grill until cooked. Keep hot for serving.

To serve, pan-fry the John Dory skin-side down in oil until golden and crisp. Then add a couple of knobs of butter, turn the fish over and cook for 2 minutes or until just translucent. Arrange the piquillos peppers in 3 points and place the char grilled courgette and aubergine in between. Place the wild rocket in the centre, add the basil and tomato concasse to the lime vierge. Place the John Dory on the rocket and drizzle the lime vierge around the garnish and on top of the fish.

Poached rhubarb and mango tart with ginger crèma cotta and caramel cage

serves 4

4 sticks of rhubarb, peeled and cut into 1cm batons

1 mango, peeled and cut into slivers 5cm long and 1mm thick

for the pastry

250g flour

175g butter

200g sugar

2 egg yolks

100ml iced water

for the crèma cotta

315ml double cream

35g sugar

1/2 vanilla pod, split in half

2 leaves of gelatine

3 or 4 stems ginger in syrup, chopped

for the stock syrup

150g sugar

150ml water

2 star anise

2 cloves

for the caramel cage

150g sugar

50ml water

1/2 teaspoon glucose

Bring the stock syrup to the boil then remove from the heat and add the rhubarb, pour into a bowl and chill. The rhubarb should be soft but retaining its shape.

To make the sweet pastry, cream the butter and sugar together and then add the egg yolks and water. Fold in the flour. When the sweet pastry has formed, wrap in cling film and chill for 30 minutes. When chilled, roll the pastry out and line 4 individual tartlet cases. Rest in the fridge for a further 20 minutes and then bake blind at 170°C/Gas Mark 3 until golden brown.

For the crèma cotta, add the sugar, cream and vanilla pod together and bring to the boil. Soak the 2 leaves of gelatine in cold water until soft. Add gelatine to the mixture and stir well. Pass through a fine sieve, add the chopped ginger and cool until set.

To create the cages, place the sugar, water and glucose in a heavy pan and boil to 153°C (using a sugar thermometer). Cool the base of the pan in cold water. Lightly grease a ladle with oil. When the caramel has cooled slightly and runs slowly off the tip of a spoon, drizzle it

around and back and forth across the ladle until you have formed a cage. Let it cool slightly, then gently twist it off and set it to rest. Continue to make a further 3 cages.

To serve, beat the ginger crèma cotta until it is smooth and broken down slightly. Fill the tartlet cases with the ginger crèma cotta and then build layers of rhubarb criss-crossing each other, with the mango slivers randomly tucked between them. Place each tart in the centre of a plate. Drizzle some of the poaching syrup around the outside. Place a sprig of mint on top to garnish. Place the cage over the tart and just before serving, dust slightly with icing sugar.

THE PRIEST HOUSE ON THE RIVER

David Cordy

Smoked garlic and chilli cured loin of English lamb

serves 4

1 bulb of garlic

1 green chilli

1 red chilli

56ml of cold pressed olive oil

salt and pepper to season

225g loin of English lamb fully trimmed to remove all fat and sinew

freshly ground black pepper

55g of freshly ground black pepper

2 shallots finely diced

110g washed rocket leaves

Start by peeling the bulb of garlic, then split the chillies in half through the middle and remove all the seeds and stalk material. Place both of these and a splash of olive oil into a food processor and using the 'pulse' button, blitz them together into a coarse paste. Using a very hot pan with a little oil, sear the lamb on all sides until it begins to colour a little. Generously season with salt and pepper and remove. Smother the paste evenly over the lamb and wrap it tightly in foil and rest in the fridge for up to 12 hours. Roast in a hot oven 220°C/Gas Mark 6 for about 15 minutes. The meat should be very pink and juicy. Allow to cool and refrigerate.

To serve, thinly slice the lamb and place in a circle around the middle of the plate. Toss the rocket leaves in the remaining olive oil and the freshly ground pepper and pile into the centre. As an option, garnish with a couple of cloves of roasted garlic for a surprisingly sweet finish.

Char grilled brill with a sauce of moules marinière and saffron

serves 4

200g - 225g portions of brill, skin removed

24 mussels, scrubbed to remove limpets and beard

8 strands of saffron

1 courgette, cut to form spaghetti-like strands

1 carrot, cut like the courgette

1 shallot

290ml double cream

150ml white wine

1 clove of garlic

55g unsalted butter

2 large potatoes, peeled

salt and pepper to season

Brush the brill with a little olive oil and lightly season. Chill and allow to rest for a couple of hours before cooking. Using a small melon-baller, scoop out 48 balls from the potatoes and blanch in boiling salted water for about 5 minutes or until just soft and refresh in iced water. Peel and finely dice the shallot and garlic.

The dish only takes about 5 minutes to cook from now.

Place the brill, face down on to a char grill pan for about 5 minutes and keep turning through 90° every 2 minutes until it is cooked. Prod the fish with your index finger to test; it should feel firm but not soggy. Meanwhile, heat a pan until searing hot and add the mussels and the white wine, cover with a tight fitting lid for 1 - 2 minutes. In a second pan, sauté the carrot and courgette spaghetti-strips in half the butter, season and cook until just soft. Lift the lid from the mussels discarding any that are still closed and pour in the cream. Reduce by half over a fierce heat. Add the rest of the butter and potatoes and gently stir until all the butter is absorbed into the sauce.

To serve, arrange the vegetable spaghetti in the middle of the plate with the brill on top. Place 3 piles of potatoes around the plate in pyramid shapes, before adding the mussels in between. Finally, drizzle the sauce over the mussels and the potatoes and serve immediately.

Iced orange soufflé with spun sugar baskets

serves 4

570ml freshly squeezed orange juice

570ml double cream

6 egg yolks

4 egg whites

560g caster sugar

1 vanilla pod

110g dark chocolate

Pour the orange juice into a pan and over a gentle heat reduce by half. Leave to cool and chill in the fridge. Whisk the egg whites and 225g of sugar into a stiff meringue. Put the egg yolks and 55g of sugar in a glass bowl over a pan of water and gently heat. Whisk like mad into pale foam, then remove from the heat immediately and keep whisking until cool. Fold in the orange juice

reduction and the meringue mix. Allow to chill for 30 minutes. On 3 layers of cling film, spoon the mixture in a long thin shape and wrap. Tie at both ends and freeze for at least 24 hours. Melt the chocolate in a bowl in the microwave in short bursts of about 10 seconds at a medium power setting, stirring each time. Remove the soufflé from the freezer, unwrap and slice at 7-8 cm lengths and dip one half in melted chocolate, sit on a tray and refreeze until ready to serve.

To make spun sugar, put 10oz of caster sugar into a clean pan with a little water. Heat and stir gently over a very low heat until it has dissolved. The sugar will start to bubble furiously and change colour. It could take anything from 10-40 minutes to reach this stage depending on the heat and the amount of water. When the colour turns to a pale brown colour, dip the bottom of the pan into a sink of cold water; this will stop the sugar from over-cooking. Grease the back of a medium sized ladle and hold in one hand. With a lot of patience, gently spoon the sugar syrup over it to create baskets.

. To serve, place the soufflé on the plate with the sugar basket, some berries and finish with a little fruit coulis.

RIBER HALL

John Bradshaw

Trio of fish with baby spinach, lobster and lobster foam

serves 4

4 x 30g portions of 3 fish, i.e. salmon, brill and sea bass

1 x lobster tail, blanched and shelled and cut into 4 portions

450g of baby spinach, blanched and refreshed

290ml lobster stock or otherwise a good fish stock

150ml double cream

12 squares of red pepper

12 spears of asparagus

chervil to garnish

Start by reducing the fish stock by half and add the cream. Season with salt, pepper and lemon juice and set aside. Place the 12 pieces of fish on a lightly oiled tray and grill. Gently toss the baby spinach in butter over heat and season. Quickly sauté the lobster in hot oil and season. Blanch the asparagus.

To serve, place a 3cm diameter cutter in the centre of a large warmed plate. Pack the cutter with the spinach. Arrange the 3 pieces of fish around the spinach. In between each piece of fish, place a square of red pepper and top with a spear of asparagus. Put a piece of lobster on top of the spinach and bring the lobster sauce back to the boil. Whisk the sauce until a froth appears on top, scoop this off with a spoon and use the foam as a sauce for the dish.

Roast breast of duck with puy lentils, black pudding and wild mushrooms with morel sauce

serves 4

4 fondant potatoes

4 duck breasts with the skin scored

110g black pudding cut into $^1/_2$ cm dice

2 large carrots cut into $^1/_2$ cm dice

85g - 110g mixed wild mushrooms

16 small morel mushrooms

12 shallots confied

12 garlic cloves confied

55g of cooked puy lentils

for the Madeira sauce

570ml beef stock

$^1/_4$ bottle of Madeira

Reduce the Madeira by half and then pour in the beef stock and continue reducing until it is the consistency of sauce.

Trim any excess fat from the duck breasts and score the skin. Place skin-side down in a hot pan and seal until the skin is golden brown, place in a hot oven for 3-4 minutes until pink. Place the fondants under a hot grill and glaze until golden. Quickly sauté the mushrooms in butter and season. Add the black pudding and diced carrots. Warm the garlic and shallots. Bring the Madeira sauce to the boil and add the morels. Reheat the lentils in a little of the sauce.

To serve, take 4 large warmed plates and place a fondant at the top of each plate. Then place a small amount of the lentils in front of the potato. Arrange the wild mushrooms, black pudding, shallots, garlic and carrots around the plate. Remove the duck breasts from the oven and slice each one into 5 pieces and place on top of the lentils. Add morel sauce and serve with extra vegetables if necessary.

Assiette of Riber desserts

Hot passion fruit soufflé; Glazed lemon tart; Red wine jelly; Mango sorbet: finished with raspberry coulis
serves 4

for the soufflé

*150ml of stock syrup
(available from good supermarkets)*

290ml of passion fruit purée

1 tablespoon of arrowroot

1 egg white and 30g of sugar

*a little extra butter and sugar for the
ramekins*

for the lemon tart

*4 individual pre-lined and baked
pastry tartlets*

juice and zest of 4 lemons

200g caster sugar

425ml double cream

6 eggs

for the red wine jelly

310ml red wine

255g sugar

4 leaves of gelatine

for the mango sorbet

500ml of puréed mango

250ml stock syrup

250ml white wine

To make the soufflé, reduce the stock syrup until a blonde caramel. Add the passion fruit purée and boil for 2 minutes. Thicken with arrowroot until quite bulky. Refrigerate until needed.

For the lemon tart, place the cream, lemon juice and zest into a pan and bring to the boil. Mix the eggs and sugar together in a bowl. Add the cream to the eggs and return to the pan. Bring back to the boil, whisking continuously until the mixture starts to thicken. Remove from the heat and pass through a fine sieve. Refrigerate until set.

For the red wine jelly, heat the wine and sugar together until the sugar dissolves. Soak the gelatine in cold water until soft. Add the gelatine to the warm wine and dissolve. Pass through a fine sieve and pour into individual moulds and add seasonal fruit if you wish. Refrigerate.

For the mango sorbet, mix all the ingredients together in a bowl. Churn in an ice cream machine until the mixture starts to freeze. When frozen place in a plastic container and freeze.

To serve, fill the pre-baked pastry tartlet moulds with the lemon mix and level off. Dust with icing sugar and glaze with a blowtorch until golden. Remove the jellies from the moulds and place onto a large plate. Add the tartlet to the plate. Whisk the egg whites and add the sugar, keep whisking until stiff and glossy. Take one tablespoon of the soufflé and gently fold in the egg whites. Fill the ramekins with the soufflé mix, level off and run your thumb around the inside rim of the ramekin. Place in a hot oven for 3-4 minutes until risen and golden brown. While the soufflés are cooking, dress the plates with berries, raspberry coulis and mint. Just before the soufflés are ready, place a quenelle of sorbet on top of the lemon tart. Remove the soufflés from the oven and add to the plates, dust with icing sugar and serve immediately.

LE POUSSIN AT PARKHILL

Alex Aitken

Cannelloni of smoked salmon

serves 6

6 leaves of smoked salmon,
cut into 6" squares

100g of smoked salmon trimmings

juice of half a lemon

1 teaspoon of creamed horseradish

1 teaspoon tomato ketchup

250ml double cream

salt and pepper

for the salsa

2 avocados, peeled, chopped and
mixed with juice of 1 lemon

4 plum tomatoes,
peeled de-seeded and chopped

1 cucumber,
peeled de-seeded and chopped

1 small chilli,
de-seeded and finely chopped

1 small bunch of coriander
finely chopped

*This is not a pasta dish at all but a
smoked salmon roll. Made in advance
it also travels very well, making it ideal
for picnics.*

First make the filling by puréeing
the smoked salmon trimmings with
the lemon juice. Put it into a mixing
bowl with the creamed horseradish
and ketchup. Whisk together into a
smooth paste. Add the double cream
a little at a time, whisking to form a
thick whipped smoked salmon cream
and chill. When chilled transfer to a
piping bag with a very large nozzle
or no nozzle at all.

Prepare the cannelloni's by first
laying a sheet of clingfilm on the
work surface. Onto the clingfilm put
1 leaf of the smoked salmon, at the
top, pipe a sausage of salmon
cream. Using the clingfilm roll the
smoked salmon leaf over the top of
itself to create the smoked salmon
roll. Keep it wrapped in the film,
twisting the ends to help keep its
shape. When finished refrigerate
until required.

To serve, mix all the ingredients
for the salsa together and arrange in
a long strip down the centre of the
plates unwrap the cannelloni and
position on top.

Terrine of roasted poussin foie gras and agen prunes

serves 8 - 10

3 whole poussins

570ml chicken stock

20 fat Agen prunes, soaked in Earl Grey tea

1 whole foie gras

1 sprig fresh thyme, stripped from the stalk

1 sprig fresh sage, finely chopped

1 sprig freshly picked tarragon, chopped

4 leaves gelatine or 3 teaspoons gelatine crystals

Roast the poussins whole until just cooked for about 15 to 20 minutes then allow to rest upside down so that all the juices are held. Allow to cool, then strip the meat from the bone keeping the breast meat whole but shredding the leg meat. Roughly chop the carcasses.

In a large saucepan, put the carcasses plus any trimmings of foie gras, herbs and cover with chicken stock. Simmer over a gentle heat to extract all the flavours. Then pass through a fine sieve and add the gelatine leaves. Reserve the liquid.

Cut the foie gras lengthways into 3 or 4 fat slices. Keep them cold. Meanwhile heat a non-stick pan until it is very hot. Season the slices of foie gras and seal very quickly in the pan and remove to a cold tray. Pour any fat and juices over the poussin leg meat.

Blanch the herbs by plunging them first into boiling hot water and then into ice-cold water. This removes the harsh bitter flavour especially from the sage but also softens them and releases their fresh flavours. Mix the chopped herbs with the shredded leg meat.

Strain the prunes, reduce the Earl Grey tea to about a tablespoon of syrup and add to the chicken stock.

Line a 1.1 litre loaf tin with clingfilm and pour a little of the gelatine stock into the bottom. Add a layer of the leg meat and herbs, top with a row of prunes and a layer of foie gras. Add a little more gelatine stock and then the poussin breasts. Continue building the terrine this way until full, topping with the gelatine stock. Cover with clingfilm and refrigerate overnight until set.

To serve, place a slice of terrine on a plate with salad dressed in light truffle oil dressing.

Hot soufflé of passion fruit

serves 4

for the soufflé sabayon

200g caster sugar

3 large egg yolks

150ml fresh passion fruit juice

for the sauce and sorbet

125g ripe mango

125g passion fruit juice

75g icing sugar

juice of 1 lemon

To make the sabayon, take a large electric mixing bowl and whisk the egg yolks and sugar to a pale cream. Heat the passion fruit juice in a thick-bottomed pan, stirring continuously so it thickens but doesn't burn. Slowly pour the yolks and sugar into the hot passion fruit juice. Continue whisking until the mixture/sabayon has cooled. At this point the mixture will keep for 2 or 3 days, however if it separates whisk again in the mixer.

For the sauce and sorbet, place all the ingredients into a liquidiser or blender and purée, then sieve, dividing the mixture into two.

For the sorbet, churn the mixture in a sorbetière, or freeze in a suitable container - stirring frequently.

For the sauce, keep until ready to serve and warm through.

To make the soufflés, butter 4 ramekins and dust with sugar. Whisk 6 egg whites into soft peaks. Whisk half into the passion fruit sabayon then gently fold in the remaining whites. Divide the mixture equally between the dishes.

Bake the souffles for 10-15 minutes until well risen.

To serve, puncture the souffle with a spoon and pour in the hot sauce. The souffle should rise again. Arrange on the plates with the sorbet as a contrast.

Juan Martin

Duck foie gras with sweetcorn pancake, peach and mango chutney and Calvados sauce

serves 4

duck foie gras – slice into 1/2" thick portions and pan fry until golden brown

for the sweetcorn pancakes allowing 2 per person

2 tablespoons warm water

1/2 teaspoon yeast

4 tablespoons of sweetcorn

$^1/_2$ teaspoon rice vinegar

1 egg

55g melted butter

180ml milk

100g flour

3 tablespoons chives

for the peach and mango chutney

500g peach and mango

$^1/_2$ cooking apple, skinned and chopped

$^1/_2$ small onion, chopped

$^1/_2$ clove garlic, chopped

$^1/_2$ tablespoon grated ginger

75g sugar

zest and juice of 1 lime

1 teaspoon salt

pinch of ground cinnamon

for the Calvados Sauce

570ml apple juice

2 tablespoons Calvados

1 tablespoon double cream

110g unsalted butter

drop of lemon juice

seasoning

For the pancakes, add the water to the yeast and cream together. Mix the flour with the egg, milk and creamed yeast, followed by the other ingredients and whisk together.

Being a yeast-based batter, allow the batter to rise and knock back. Cook the pancakes individually in a medium hot pan with olive oil for approximately 1 minute, each side.

To make the peach and mango chutney, combine all the ingredients except for the sugar. Cook in a pan on a medium heat until tender and then add the sugar. Continue cooking a further 10 minutes.

For the Calvados sauce, reduce the apple juice to 4 tablespoons, add the cream and whisk in the unsalted butter with the Calvados, lemon juice and seasoning and liquidise prior to serving.

To serve, place a portion of warm chutney in the centre of 4 large white plates. Add the pancake and top with sautéed foie gras. Drizzle the bowl with Calvados sauce.

Tournedos of Scottish fillet steak with braised oxtail, seasonal vegetables and red wine sauce

serves 4

4 x 170g Tournedos of fillet steak

for the braised oxtail

1 thick part of an oxtail bone

3-4 leaves of green cabbage, blanched

55g bacon, cut into pieces and blanched

55g mushrooms

1 teaspoon fresh herbs

2 shallots, sliced

for the red wine sauce

400ml red wine

1 shallot

2-3 mushrooms

1 clove garlic

sprig of thyme

bay leaf

250ml chicken stock

50g butter

Sweat the shallots and mushrooms and add the bacon and herbs. Line the oxtail with the cabbage and stuff it with the other ingredients. Roll the oxtail and tie in 2cm intervals. Place into an ovenproof dish and braise in red wine until cooked for 3-4 hours at 170°C/Gas Mark 3. Remove the oxtail and reduce the liquid.

For the red wine sauce, sweat the shallot, mushrooms and garlic add the wine and chicken stock with bay leaf and thyme and reduce to 150ml. Whisk in the butter at the end.

White chocolate tear filled with white chocolate marquise and brandied cherries

serves 8

for the chocolate tear

125g white chocolate

for the filling
– white chocolate marquise

430ml double cream

225g white chocolate

75g/approximately 2¹/₂ egg whites

110g caster sugar

2¹/₂ leaves gelatine

To make the white chocolate tear, melt the chocolate in a bowl over a pan of simmering water like a Bain Marie, carefully pour enough for 1 portion on to a sheet of acetate, and mould into a tear shape. Leave a hole in the middle for the filling. Repeat, and chill to set.

Boil the sugar in a little water to 188°C (soft ball). Whisk the egg whites to a stiff peak and pour on the sugar. Soak the gelatine and dissolve in the sugar pan. Add this to the egg whites and mix until cold.

Semi-whip the cream. Melt the chocolate in a Bain Marie. Do not allow to boil. Lightly fold the cream into the egg whites and then the melted chocolate. Ensure the chocolate is cool.

To serve, fill the tear half way and place in it a well drained brandied cherry. Pipe to the top and smooth with a palette knife. Place in the fridge and allow to set.

THE ATLANTIC HOTEL

Ken Healy

Foie gras tarte tatin

serves 4

4 x 1g slice of foie gras

4 Granny Smith apples

*4 discs puff pastry,
100mm in diameter*

4 teaspoons white sugar

80g butter

4 teaspoons raspberry vinegar

seasoning

salad leaves

Peel the apples, core and cut each into 8 pieces. Caramelise with the sugar and butter in a hot pan. Arrange the caramelised apples in 4 moulds (100mm) with their juices. Cover with a puff pastry disc and cook for 15-20 minutes at 180°C/Gas Mark 4 until golden brown.

Season the foie gras and cook in a very hot dry pan, colour on both sides and deglaze with raspberry vinegar. Cook until pink and soft.

To serve, unmould the tarts and place the cooked foie gras on the apple, pour over some of the cooking juices and serve with dressed salad leaves.

Blanquette of lobster

serves 4

4 x 500g fresh lobsters

2 small carrots

1 small leek

4 shallots

50g salted butter

20ml dry white wine

10ml Noilly Prat

70ml double cream

1 packet fresh noodles/spaghetti

salt and pepper

freshly picked herbs

Cook the lobsters in boiling water for 12 minutes. Remove from the pan and allow to cool. Cut away the shell, keeping the head and tail (washed) for garnish. Slice the lobster tail in half lengthways and clean. Peel the vegetables and cut into slices 3mm thick. Warm the butter in a pan, soften the vegetables, then add the wine and Noilly Prat, season and cook until soft. Add the cream and bring to the boil. Reduce the heat, add the lobster and simmer until hot but do not boil.

To serve, cook the pasta, drain, season and place in the middle of 4 warm plates or bowls. Arrange the washed lobster shells as garnish. Taste the lobster for seasoning, add the fresh herbs and divide between the 4 plates. Pour the sauce and vegetables over. Serve with a side salad.

Chocolate and fresh berry tart

serves 4

175g flour

65g diced soft butter

1 whole egg

5g caster sugar

10ml water

pinch of salt

300g mixed berries

for the chocolate filling

175g dark chocolate, chopped

200ml whipping cream

20g liquid glucose

40g butter, softened

To make the sweet pastry base, place the flour on a work surface and rub in the diced butter. Add sugar and salt. Make a well, add the egg and draw into the flour until crumbly. Add water to bind and knead until smooth. Wrap in polythene and put into the fridge for 2-3 hours. Line a round tin 150mm x 150mm with the pastry. Cover with cling film and weigh down with baking beans or rice. Bake blind at 200°C/Gas Mark 6 until lightly brown. Remove the cling film and return to the oven until golden brown all over.

To make the filling, heat the cream in a saucepan to boiling point. Pour onto the chopped chocolate. Stir in the liquid glucose and butter.

Place the mixed berries into the pastry case, keep a few back for decoration. Fill the pastry case to the top with the chocolate mixture, allow to settle and place in the fridge until required.

To serve, slice the tart with a warm sharp knife, arrange on the plates and decorate with berries.

MALLORY COURT

Steve Love

Seared scallops wrapped in smoked salmon with a pea velouté sauce

serves 4

12 x 40g scallops
12 thinly sliced strips of smoked salmon
1/2 iceberg lettuce
1 large onion

570ml chicken stock
300g peas
150ml double cream
2 plum tomatoes, skinned, deseeded and diced

50g unsalted butter
100ml good quality olive oil
1 lemon
4 sprigs of chervil

Peel the lemon and juice, place in good quality olive oil and bring to approximately 75°C and allow to cool and infuse. Pass through a fine sieve.

Finely shred the onion. Place into a pan with half the chicken stock, cover and cook slowly for about 45 minutes or until the onions are completely soft. Remove the lid and reduce the cooking liquor and the onions until almost dry. Reserve for later use. This can be done in advance and chilled.

Remove the orange coral from the scallops and wrap the strips of smoked salmon around, leaving the top and bottom visible. Cut any trimmings from the smoked salmon into fine strips for use later as a garnish.

Take the remainder of the chicken stock and bring to the boil and add the peas. Cook quickly to keep the colour. When cooked

remove 1/4 of the peas and refresh in iced water to garnish later. Place the rest of the peas with the chicken stock, a dash of double cream and a knob of butter into a blender and process until smooth. Pass this through a fine sieve and cool.

Finely chiffonarde, (coarsely shred) the iceberg lettuce.

Place the pea mixture into a pan and warm through. Adjust the consistency with a little cream and possibly more stock (being careful not to lose the flavour or colour of the liquid). Adjust the seasoning with salt and pepper.

In a separate pan, place 50ml of double cream and a knob of butter. Bring to the boil and add the onions (but not any excess liquid) and the lettuce. Cook slowly for 2-3 minutes until the lettuce is soft.

Season the scallops with pepper

only, as the smoked salmon is salty enough. Pan-fry the scallops in a very hot pan with a little olive oil and a knob of butter. Turn the scallops, making sure they have browned on each side but slightly pink on the inside. Squeeze with lemon juice and drain onto a clean cloth.

Heat the peas retained for the garnish plus the tomato dice in a little butter, season with salt and pepper.

To serve, place the onion and lettuce mixture into the middle of a warm plate. Surround with 3 small piles of the extra smoked salmon cut from the trimmings. Put 1 scallop on top of each pile. Sauce the rest of the plate. Drain the pea and tomato garnish onto a clean cloth and share equally. Finish with a swirl of the lemon oil (mix well before use) and a sprig of chervil.

Seared scallops wrapped in smoked salmon with a pea velouté sauce

Braised blade of beef with smoked bacon, lentils and garlic cabbage

Braised blade of beef with smoked bacon, lentils and garlic cabbage

serves 4

1 blade of good quality beef

1 bottle of red wine

1.71 litres (3 pints)
of veal or beef stock

¹/₂ Savoy cabbage

2 cloves of garlic

2 medium Maris Piper potatoes

2 medium Desiré potatoes

50ml double cream

50g lentil de puy

150g pancetta or smoked streaky
bacon

50ml olive oil

2 medium carrots

1 sprig of thyme

80g broad beans

100 butter

50ml sunflower oil

Take the blade of beef and trim away the excess sinew. Secure with some string. Season with the salt and pepper. Pre-heat a frying pan, add some sunflower oil and seal the blade on all sides until brown. Put the blade into a large casserole. Peel and quarter the carrots and onions and with the red wine, stock and thyme add to the casserole. Cover with a lid and bring to the boil on the stove and put into the oven 150°C/Gas Mark 2 for approximately 2 hours. (Do not allow it to boil in the oven). When it is cooked, a knife will go into the meat very easily. Remove from the container and

allow to drain and cool slightly on a wire rack. Remove the string and wrap in clingfilm. Pull tight and secure each end with string. Hang upright in the fridge (this is best done in advance so that the beef can set). Skim any excess fat from the stock and reduce until sauce consistency. Keep for later.

To make the potato crisp, peel and grate the Maris Piper potato. Dry away any excess moisture. Season with salt and pepper. Take a small frying pan with olive oil and spread into 4 discs and cook on a moderate heat until light brown in colour. Turn over and carry on cooking until browned on both sides. Allow to drain on a clean cloth or kitchen paper.

Cook the desiré potatoes in salted water, slowly with the skin on. Drain, remove skins and pass through a fine sieve. Bring 50ml double cream and a knob of butter to the boil and reduce slightly and add potatoes. Combine together and adjust seasoning. Keep for later.

Cut the pancetta into thin strips, grill 12 slices until crisp. Cut the rest into very small lardons and fry in olive oil until nice and crispy. Strain, keeping the excess oil for later.

Simmer the lentils in water with some of the pancetta trimmings and a sprig of thyme. Cook until soft making sure that the lentils are covered with water at all times and not allowed to boil. Drain and discard the thyme and pancetta trimmings.

Finely shred the Savoy cabbage and cook in salted boiling water, refresh in iced water, drain and dry. Put 2 cloves of garlic (peeled and cut in half) dry into a pan with 2 knobs of butter, heat until melted and bubbling. Strain off the garlic and pour the butter over the dry cabbage and save for later.

To serve, slice the chilled blade of beef into 4 nice size pieces. Place onto a greased baking tray with a knob of butter on top. When re-heated carefully place into the sauce and coat. Warm the plates and put the potato purée into a piping bag. Pipe onto the plates in a small swirl pointing upwards. Reheat the cabbage in a pan on the stove. Place into a ring mould slightly smaller than the potato crisp. Remove the mould and place the potato crisp on top of the cabbage and put the beef on top. Pass the sauce through a fine sieve and add the crispy bacon lardons, lentil and broad beans to the sauce. Sauce the plate putting a little over the top of the beef. Put the grilled pancetta on the potato purée and finish with a drizzle of pancetta flavoured oil.

Trio of lemon desserts

serves 4

for the lemon chiffon mousse

125ml water

60g caster sugar

for the pastry cream

4 large egg yolks

35ml water

25g cornflour

60g caster sugar

grated zest of 1 lemon

2¹/₂ leaves of gelatine

70ml water

100ml lemon juice

115g caster sugar

4 large egg whites

Mix 125ml of water and 60g of caster sugar together in a pan. Bring to the boil and simmer until dissolved. For the pastry cream, mix the egg yolks, water, cornflour and 60g caster sugar and the zest of 1 lemon together and add to the syrup, stirring continuously on a low heat until it thickens. Remove from the heat. Soak the gelatine leaves in a little water with the lemon juice and add to the pastry cream while it is still hot, allow to cool. Whisk 115g caster sugar and the egg whites into stiff peaks and gently fold into the pastry cream also, careful not to knock the air out of the meringue. Spoon into a suitable size mould and allow to set in the fridge.

Lemon sorbet

500ml water

340g caster sugar

6 lemon, grated and juiced

Mix the water and the sugar together in a pan. Bring to the boil and simmer until dissolved. Add the juice and the grated lemon and allow to infuse whilst it cools down. Churn in an ice-cream machine. Remove and keep in a sealed container in the freezer.

Glazed lemon tart

225g plain flour

pinch of salt

150g unsalted butter (room temperature)

75g caster sugar

1 egg yolk

1 whole egg

1 grated lemon

for the lemon mix

6 lemons

9 whole eggs

400g caster sugar

300ml double cream

Sift the flour and salt, rub in the butter until mixture resembles breadcrumbs. Mix in the sugar, the egg yolk, egg and the lemon. Mix

together, wrap in clingfilm and refrigerate for about half an hour before use. Roll out the pastry and line an 8 or 10" greased flan case or ring, leave a little bit of pastry overlapping the edge to allow for shrinkage. Fill with baking beans on a sheet of greaseproof paper and refrigerate for about 1 hour. Pre-heat the oven to 180°C/Gas Mark 4 and bake the case until the sides are golden brown, approximately 15-20 minutes. Remove the beans and paper, brush the pastry with an egg yolk and return to the oven for a further 5 minutes. Remove and slightly cool. Reduce the oven temperature to 120°C/Gas Mark 2.

Wash the lemons, grate 3, juice all of them and strain. Beat the sugar and eggs together until smooth. Add the cream and lemon, mixture and mix well. Pour into the pastry case and cook for approximately 30-35 minutes in the cooler oven until set.

To serve, de-mould the chiffon onto the plate. Cut a wedge of tart and sprinkle with caster sugar and caramelise lightly with a blow torch (or dust with icing sugar) and arrange next to the chiffon. Ball the lemon sorbet and serve this on top of some chopped nuts to secure it to the plate.

Peter Malcher

Chargrilled salmon with asparagus, herb blinis, crème fraîche, caviar, and basil oil

serves 4

1x 560g salmon fillet, skin on and de-scaled

12 asparagus spears

200g crème fraîche, mixed with chopped chives

15g Sevruga caviar

1 centre of a curly endive

4 sprigs of chervil

for the herb blinis

2 tablespoons of finely chopped soft herbs

165g brown flour

165g strong white flour

330ml warm milk

300g clarified butter

15g yeast

6 egg yolks

6 egg whites

salt and pepper

for the basil oil

1 bunch of basil

250ml olive oil

250mm grape seed oil

salt and pepper

To make the blinis, warm the milk to blood temperature and whisk in the yeast and egg yolks. Sieve the 2 flours together with the salt into a bowl. Make a well in the middle and pour in the milk mixture and gradually mix together. Cover with cling film and place in a warm area for approximately 1 hour to prove. Add the chopped mixed herbs. Fold in the melted butter then fold in the whisked egg whites. Heat 4 blinis pans with a little olive oil and ladle some mixture into each. Cook for approximately 3 minutes on each side and put to one side.

Make the basil oil by blanching the leaves in boiling salted water and refreshing under cold water, place in a liquidiser with the oils, salt and pepper and blitz for 2 minutes.

Trim the bottom of the asparagus and peel off the lower leaves, blanch in boiling salted water and refresh in ice-cold water.

Cut the salmon into 8 equal slices, approximately half an inch thick. Season with salt and pepper, coat in olive oil and char grill for 1 minute on both sides. Then grill the asparagus.

To serve, place the blinis in the centre of the plate. Toss the curly endive in a little olive oil, season and place on top of the blinis. Lay 2 pieces of salmon on the curly endive with 3 asparagus spears, quenelle some crème fraîche with 2 dessertspoons and place on top. Put a little caviar and chervil sprig to finish on the crème fraîche, drizzle basil oil around and serve.

Roast fillet of Scottish beef with an oxtail ravioli, sautéed beef marrow and horseradish cream

serves 4

olive oil

4 x 170g - 200g beef fillets

500g picked and washed spinach

2kg beef marrowbones, marrow pushed out

2 tablespoons roughly chopped flat parsley

for the oxtail

2kg cut oxtail

100g each of roughly chopped carrot, celery, leek and onion

1 bay leaf

thyme

1 garlic clove

black peppercorns

1 litre of red wine

2 litres of veal stock

for the pasta

500g strong white flour

2 eggs

3 egg yolks

1 tablespoon white wine vinegar

1 tablespoon olive oil

for the horseradish cream

1/2 fresh horseradish stick

1 tablespoon chopped English parsley

1 tablespoon coarse grain mustard

2 tablespoons white wine vinegar

1/2 litre double cream

for the shallot marmalade

500g sliced shallots

1 tablespoon olive oil

First place the oxtail and roughly cut vegetables in a container with the garlic, herbs and red wine and marinade for 24 hours in the fridge.

The following day strain the red wine from the oxtail and vegetables and keep to one side.

Season the meat of the oxtail with salt and pepper and brown in a frying pan with a little olive oil. When an even brown colour, add the vegetables and carry on frying for another 5 minutes and place in an earthenware casserole dish. Add the red wine marinade and reduce by half over the heat. Then add the veal stock so it just covers the oxtail and bring to the boil. Place a tight fitting lid on the dish and put in a preheated oven to 160°C/Gas Mark 2¹/₂ for about 2-3 hours or until the meat falls away from the bone. Once cooked, remove from the oven and cool down. Strain the meat and keep the sauce to one side for later. Flake the meat into a separate bowl insuring there are no small bones in it. Add the roughly chopped flat parsley, shallot marmalade and a couple of teaspoons of reserved sauce to moisten. While the oxtail is in the oven you can make the pasta, marmalade and horseradish cream.

Put the flour in a food processor then mix the eggs with vinegar and oil. Turn the processor on and gently pour the egg mix into the flour until it comes together. Put the dough on a floured table and knead for 5 minutes until smooth. Wrap in cling film and chill for 1 hour.

Place the sliced shallots in a heavy-bottomed pan with a little olive oil and on a low heat, cook until the shallots start to caramelise in their own juices. Add to the oxtail mixture.

Peel the horseradish and wash. Finely grate the horseradish into a bowl with the mustard, parsley and vinegar. Whip the cream in a separate bowl until stiff and fold into horseradish mix, season with salt and pepper. Keep in the fridge.

Using a pasta machine, roll out the dough, gradually turning the machine down to the finest setting (the pasta should be translucent). Cut out 4 x 6cm discs and put some oxtail mix in the centre. Cut out 4 x 5cm disks and cover the mixture, bring the bottom sides up and press the edges together to seal.

Warm the reserved sauce and check consistency. Pass through muslin into a clean pan, whisk in a knob of butter and keep warm.

Seal beef fillets all over and cook to required preference. Sauté spinach in a little butter, olive oil and season, place on a cloth to squeeze excess liquid out. Blanch ravioli in boiling, salted water.

To serve, put a beef fillet to one side on the plate and the spinach in a cutter on the other side. Place ravioli on top of the spinach. Quickly sauté the beef marrow and put on top of the ravioli. Make a quenelle of horseradish cream with 2 spoons and place on top of the beef. Pour sauce around and serve.

Vanilla pudding soufflé with a blood orange sorbet

serves 4

150g caster sugar

350g cream cheese

4 egg yolks

4 egg whites

1 vanilla pod (seed only)

for the blood orange sorbet

500ml blood orange juice, freshly squeezed

150g caster sugar

50g liquid glucose

for the orange garnish

1 seedless orange, segmented

juice of 1 orange

50g caster sugar

Grease 6 ramekin dishes with melted butter, freeze and repeat the process.

In an electric mixer using the beater, smooth 50g caster sugar, the cream cheese, egg yolks and vanilla pod seeds. Scrape into a round-bottomed bowl and place into the fridge. Whisk the egg whites and 100g caster sugar into soft peaks. Fold the meringue carefully into the cheese mixture. Fill the ramekins to the top and smooth with a pallet knife. Place in a pre-heated oven set at 170°C/Gas Mark 3 for 20-22 minutes.

For the blood orange sorbet, place all the ingredients into a pan. Bring to the boil then allow to cool.

Using an ice-cream machine, churn the sorbet until thick and slushy; try not to over churn, as the sorbet will lose its colour. Set in a freezer for 2-3 hours.

To make the garnish, place all the ingredients into a thick-bottomed pan. Bring to the boil then reduce to simmer for 10-15 minutes until the segments begin to shine. Allow to cool.

To serve, dust the soufflés with icing sugar and arrange on the plates with the orange garnish and a quenelle of blood orange sorbet.

LANGSHOTT MANOR

Stephen Toward

Poached native lobster Maultaschen ravioli with cucumber broth

Poached native lobster Maultaschen ravioli with cucumber broth

serves 2

for the Maultaschen/ravioli filling

1 prepared lobster tail and 2 claws

1 slice of fresh white bread made into crumbs

150g white and brown crabmeat

1/2 egg

salt and pepper

lemon juice

flat leaf parsley, finely snipped

for the various pasta

250g flour

2-3 egg yolks

1 tablespoon tomato purée – red pasta

1 tablespoon puréed spinach – green pasta

1g powdered saffron – yellow pasta

for the cucumber and chive broth

100ml white wine

1 shallot, finely chopped

1/2 clove of garlic

1/2 lemon, juiced

1/2 stick of lemon grass, crushed

250ml vegetable stock

1 bay leaf

cucumber trimmings

150g cold butter

To make the ravioli, cut the lobster tail in half lengthways and remove the black centre cord and set aside with the claws. Place the crab in a bowl and add the breadcrumbs, lemon juice, parsley, egg, salt and pepper. Mix until incorporated together and place in the fridge.

For the pastas, place the flour in a food processor and add the egg yolk and required ingredient to colour the mixture. The pasta should resemble coarse crumbs and stick together when pressed, a little water maybe added if required. Remove the dough, wrap in cling film and refrigerate. Repeat the process until all the colours are made. Roll out on the thickest setting of a pasta machine. Cut strips of approximately 1cm wide. Repeat the process until all the colours are cut. Place under cling film. Egg wash 1 side of a strip. Place the next coloured pasta on the egg-washed side. Repeat until you have 2 colours of each, (i.e. red, green, yellow, red, green, yellow). Flour each side and cling film for about 5 minutes. Transfer to the pasta machine and roll out to the thinnest setting, take care you may need to flour it to prevent it sticking. Refrigerate again until required.

For the cucumber broth, melt a knob of butter and gently sweat off the shallot, garlic, cucumber, bay leaf and lemon grass. Add the white

wine, stock and lemon juice. Cook until nearly all the liquid has evaporated. Add the cream and a few knobs of butter one at a time. Whisk rapidly and continuously until smooth. Pass through a fine sieve and adjust the seasoning.

To make the ravioli, roll out the pasta on the finest setting of the pasta machine. Take a 5" square of the striped pasta, lightly egg-wash around the edge and put 1 tablespoon of the crab filling in the centre. Put a piece of the lobster tail on top but do not push down too hard. Lay another square of pasta on top and seal the edges with your fingers. Then take a 4" round cutter and cut out the ravioli shapes. Clear away excess pasta dough and discard. Blanch in boiling water.

To serve, gently warm the lobster claws. Place the warm cucumber broth on the bottom of a warm bowl and place a ravioli on top. Garnish with a lobster claw and serve straight away.

Crackling milk pork with baked garden beetroot and green pickled peppercorn sauce

serves 4

4 x 200g pieces of suckling pork

300g beetroot, cooked and puréed

300g broccoli, cooked and puréed

300g young carrots, cooked and puréed

1 litre chicken stock

2 bay leaves

garlic clove

sprig of thyme

sprig of rosemary

Maldon sea salt

vegetable oil

1 tablespoon pickled green peppercorns

1 small cooking apple

a small amount of unsalted butter

Pre-heat the oven to 200°C/Gas Mark 6-7. Score the skin of the pork and rub in a small amount of sea salt. Place in a roasting tin with the roughly chopped apple, thyme, rosemary and garlic. Put in the oven for about 30 minutes or until crispy crackling starts to appear.

Meanwhile, heat up the puréed vegetables (these can be made a day in advance) and place somewhere warm until required.

Remove the pork from the oven and rest to one side. Place the roasting tray on the heat and reduce the liquor until the liquid has evaporated. Pour off any excess fat and add the chicken stock - reduce by about three quarters. Strain through a sieve and reduce further. Add a small amount of butter and the crushed pickled peppercorns until thickened.

To serve, place the warmed purées onto hot plates with the pork and finish with the sauce.

Terzetto of finest Swiss chocolate

for the white chocolate Pernod parfait

150g white chocolate

50g sugar

7 egg yolks

500ml whipped cream

150ml Pernod

for the tuile baskets

6 egg whites

225g icing sugar

225g flour

150g melted butter

for the ice cream

500ml milk

500ml double cream

200g sugar

15 egg yolks

a handful of milk chocolate

for the chocolate drink

200ml full cream milk

1 tablespoon whipping cream

vanilla pod, cinnamon stick and a pinch of mace

pinch of salt

pinch of freshly ground black pepper

50g chocolate

for the milk chocolate mousse

1 egg

1 egg yolk

150g milk chocolate

150ml double cream

For the white chocolate and Pernod parfait, whisk the sugar and yolks in a bowl over a pan of boiling water until it thickens. Add the melted chocolate to the mixture and leave to cool. Add the Pernod. Whisk the cream until it thickens and fold into the egg mixture. Transfer to a mould and place in the freezer.

To make the tuile biscuits, sieve the flour and icing sugar together and mix in the egg whites. Add the melted butter when cool, into the mixture. Bake in a gentle oven until lightly golden and cool on a rack.

For the ice cream, boil the milk and cream together. Whisk the yolks and sugar together. Pour the milk over the sugar and eggs and leave to cool down. Place in an ice cream machine and freeze. When nearly frozen, add the melted chocolate and return to the freezer.

For the chocolate drink, put the milk and cream with the spices, salt and pepper in a saucepan, bring to the point where tiny bubbles appear around the edge of the pan. Put the chocolate in a bowl and stand in very hot water. Pour the milk over chocolate and stir until it has melted. Let it stand for a few minutes. Strain into a heated jug.

To make the milk chocolate mousse, crack the egg and egg yolk into a bowl and whisk over a pan of boiling water until thick. Remove from the heat. Melt the chocolate in a bowl and pour into the egg mixture – leave to cool. Whip the cream to a soft peak and pour into the chocolate mixture. Transfer into moulds and leave in the fridge to set for 2 hours.

To serve, arrange individual portions of each dessert on the plates, garnish with the tuile biscuits and finish with the chocolate drink.

SHEEN FALLS LODGE

Chris Farrell

Cappuccino of wild mushrooms

serves 2

2 finely diced shallots

50g mixed wild mushrooms – chanterelles, black trumpets, boletus or similar (Dried will do if fresh are not available)

25g button mushrooms

250ml chicken stock

250ml cream

25g unsalted butter

If using dried mushrooms, soak for 1 hour in warm water and strain. Sweat off the shallots with a little butter and add the mushrooms. Cook on a low heat for about 5 minutes. Deglaze the pan by adding the chicken stock, reduce by half and add the cream.

Cook for a few minutes only, strain, discard the mushrooms and blend with a hand blender and use the foam to give the Cappuccino effect. Season to taste and serve in a small demitasse cup.

Squab pigeon with fondant potato, buttered spinach and confit of garlic

serves 2

2 squab pigeons, wishbones removed

10 cloves of garlic, cooked in olive oil at 140°C/Gas Mark 1 for 40 minutes

50g spinach leaves, cooked in boiling salted water and strained

1 plum tomato, skinned, deseeded and diced

25g wild mushrooms for garnish (optional)

50ml veal or poultry jus

for the fondant potato

4 medium sized potatoes such as Kerr Pinks

250g salted butter

1 dessertspoon of Madeira

Maldon salt

Peel the potatoes, top and tail them evenly and cut vertically with a round pastry cutter. Check that they are all the same height and pat dry with kitchen paper. Put some salted butter in a thick-bottomed sauté pan and bring the butter to a foam state, add the potatoes. Deglaze the pot by adding a dessertspoon of Madeira. Cook slowly on a low/medium heat, check regularly to ensure they do not over cook. Season with Maldon salt.

Seal the pigeon in a frying pan for long enough to develop a good colour. Place in a hot oven for 5 minutes or for longer if you prefer it well done. The potatoes can be put in the oven with the pigeon to keep warm. Meanwhile, heat the spinach with a little butter and season to taste. Sweat off the wild mushrooms in a hot pan and season to taste. The confit of garlic can be heated with the pigeon or on a separate tray in the oven. Place the jus and diced tomato in a pot to heat.

To serve, place the spinach in a mould on a plate and the confit of garlic around. Remove the breasts from the pigeon crown and arrange on top of the spinach. Keep the spinach and pigeon to the front of the plate and place the fondant potatoes behind it. Dress the plate with the sauce and the wild mushrooms.

Caramel soufflé

serves 2

for the crème patissière

6 egg yolks

20g sugar

30g flour

20g corn flour

200ml milk

for the caramel

200g sugar

25ml water

Whisk the eggs and sugar, add the flour and corn flour and whisk in the milk. Cook for 5-10 minutes over a gentle heat until the flour is cooked. To make the caramel, dissolve the sugar in the water to the caramel stage using a sugar thermometer. If you haven't got a thermometer, cook until light brown in colour. Add to the crème patissiere. Coat the inside of the soufflé moulds with soft butter and then with granulated sugar. Spoon in the mixture to just below the top of the mould. Cook for 10-15 minutes at 175°C/Gas Mark 4^{1}/$_{2}$ and serve immediately.

MATFEN HALL

Craig McMeeken

Baked cheddar cheese and spinach soufflé

serves 12

900ml milk

1 studded onion

3 cloves

1 bay leaf

1/4 teaspoon ground nutmeg

150g unsalted butter

150g plain flour

12 eggs

500g grated mature cheddar

200g baby spinach

Bring the milk to the boil with the studded onion, bay leaf and ground nutmeg. Once the milk has boiled, remove from the heat and stand to allow all the flavours to infuse.

In a separate pan, melt the butter and add the flour, cook out the roux and slowly start to incorporate the milk until a smooth white sauce is obtained. Add the grated cheddar cheese to the sauce and mix through. Remove the sauce and allow to cool, and then mix in the egg yolks and blanched chopped spinach.

Whisk the egg whites into soft peaks. Gently fold the egg whites into the cheese sauce. The mix will have doubled in volume.

Line the moulds with the softened butter and place back in the fridge to set and when chilled, repeat the process again. Finish with a coat of finely grated Parmesan cheese. Carefully fill the moulds and cook in a roasting tin half-filled with water i.e. a Bain Marie at 140°C/Gas Mark 1 for 20 minutes.

Once cooked, remove from the moulds and put on a tray in the oven at 180°C/Gas Mark 4 for 7 minutes until the soufflés are browned evenly. In a pan, heat 1/4 pint of double cream and 250g grated Parmesan and pour over the soufflés and sprinkle with Parmesan. Place under the grill until glazed and serve.

Brill in red wine with confit shallots and salsify

serves 4

4 x 200g fillets of Brill

500g potatoes

125g unsalted butter

5 tablespoons double cream

2 teaspoons chopped parsley

3 salsify

4 button shallots

2 teaspoons lemon juice

400ml seasoned red wine

Gently simmer the potatoes until tender, drain all the water and put back on the stove- top to dry. Mash and press through a sieve, adding the unsalted butter and double cream whilst still warm.

Peel the shallots and sauté in a hot oiled pan, finish with a little butter. Peel the salsify and cook until evenly coloured.

Marinate the Brill fillets for 24 hours in red wine, salt and pepper and finely diced shallot. When ready to serve, heat the marinade and plunge the fish in for 2-3 minutes. Sauté the spinach with butter, salt and pepper and when cooked, absorb the excess liquid with a cloth or kitchen paper.

To serve, push a portion of spinach into a mould on the plate and sit the fish gently on top. Quenelle the mash, sprinkle with chopped parsley and arrange next to the fish with the salsify and shallots. Garnish with flat parsley. Reduce the cooking liquor with a little basic fish stock, thicken sauce by whisking in cold diced butter and drizzle around the plate.

Warm liquid centred chocolate cake with coconut ice cream

serves 4

for the chocolate cake

500g dark chocolate

500g butter

10 eggs

10 egg yolks

300g sugar

50g Flour

Butter 20 non-stick pudding moulds, then coat with cornflour. Whisk the eggs, egg yolks and sugar: the mix will almost double in volume.

Slowly mix in the flour. Once all the flour has been incorporated add the melted dark chocolate and butter.

Pour mixture straight into the pre-lined moulds and cook in oven at 180°C for 8 minutes. Take out of oven and allow to rest for 2 minutes; the cake will release from the sides of the mould and turn out cleanly.

Turn out and place in centre of plate. Simply serve with a ball of coconut ice-cream on top end a sprig of mint.

for the coconut ice cream

20 egg yolks

750g sugar

1 litre double cream

1 litre milk

500g puréed coconut

Whisk the egg yolks and sugar until the mixture reaches ribbon stage and the mix lightens in colour.

Warm the milk and cream and add to the sugar and egg mix; take the mix to just before boiling point.

Remove to a clean container and cool before churning.

THE PRIORY BAY HOTEL

David Whiffen

Warm skate and walnut salad

Priory Bay pheasant

Hazelnut and blueberry bakewell

Warm skate and walnut salad

Serves 6

6 x 150g skate wings,
boned and filleted

170g chopped walnuts

2 large carrots,
peeled and cut into julienne strips
and soaked in iced water

1 medium leek,
peeled and cut into julienne strips
and soaked in iced water

300g washed mixed lettuce leaves

60g shallots, chopped

$1/2$ bunch chives cut into baton sized
pieces

55g butter

1 orange, segmented for garnish

for the dressing

90ml olive oil

56ml cider vinegar

28ml walnut oil

30g whole grain mustard

Mix the lettuce, shallots, 85g of the walnuts, and dressing together.

Pan-fry the skate in the butter until golden brown and season with salt and pepper.

Put the remaining walnuts in a medium oven and roast until lightly browned.

To serve, place the salad in the centre of the plates, top with pan-fried skate and garnish with carrots, leeks, chives and roasted walnuts.

Priory Bay pheasant

serves 6

3 whole pheasants, the legs and thighs removed, with the bone taken out and the thighs ready for stuffing

225g chicken and girolle mousse

290ml red wine sauce

450g mashed potatoes

340g girolles, for garnish

340g vegetables for garnish – carrots, brussel sprouts, swede – glazed in butter and sugar

225g butter, unsalted

for the chicken and girolle mousse

225g breast of chicken

2 whole eggs

290ml double cream

285g girolles, cooked in a little port

for the mashed potato

675g good potatoes

225g butter, diced

290ml double cream, warmed

for the red wine sauce

1 bottle red wine

285g shallots, peeled and cut in half

110g butter

1.14 litres chicken stock

110g mushrooms

15g thyme

1/2 head of garlic

To make the mousse, blend the chicken to a paste with the eggs and a good pinch of salt. Add the cream a little at a time. Put the mixture in a bowl on ice and add the cooked girolles and mix well. The mousse will keep in the fridge for 24 hours.

Stuff the legs and thighs with the mousse, wrap them in cling film and poach for 15 minutes and then let them cool. Place the pheasant breasts on the bone with a rasher of bacon on top to keep them moist and roast in a moderate oven for 12-18 minutes. Be careful not to overcook them or they will dry out. When the pheasant is cooked, remove the breasts from the bones and keep warm.

Roughly chop the bones and brown in a little butter, add the red wine sauce and cook for 10-15 minutes. Strain through muslin or a fine sieve, add some butter to finish and keep warm.

Sauté the girolles in a little butter and add to the sauce.

For the red wine sauce, brown the shallots in a little butter, add the mushrooms, thyme and garlic and sweat for 2-3 minutes. Then add all the wine and reduce by 3/4 on a high heat. Add the stock and reduce again to 290ml. Strain through muslin or a fine sieve and keep warm.

Wash and peel the potatoes and cook in salted water. Drain and mash, add the diced butter and the cream and mix well. Add salt and pepper to taste.

To serve, cut the breasts into 2–3 pieces and place on top of a portion of mashed potato on the plates. Cut the leg in 2 at the joint, stand the drumstick up and slice the thigh into 4 or 5 pieces and place at the bottom of the drumstick. Garnish the plate with the vegetables and sauce.

Hazelnut and blueberry bakewell

serves 4

225g sugar paste
(available from a good delicatessen)

55g apricot glaze
(apricot jam, warmed and sieved)

225g blueberries

for the sugar pastry

1 medium egg

50g sugar

125g butter

200g soft flour

a pinch of salt

for the frangipane

110g butter

55g ground hazelnuts

55g flour

2 eggs

110g sugar

To make the pastry, sieve the flour and salt and lightly rub in the butter to a sandy texture. Mix the sugar and egg until dissolved. Make a well in the centre and add the sugar and beaten egg. Gradually incorporate the flour and margarine and lightly mix to a smooth paste. Rest the pastry before using.

For the frangipane, cream the sugar and butter together and gradually beat in the eggs. Mix in the ground hazelnuts and flour and mix lightly.

Line a flan ring with the sugar pastry 2-3mm thick and pierce the bottom with a fork. Spread the blueberries thinly on the bottom and cover with frangipane. Bake in a moderate oven at 200-220°C/Gas Mark 6-7 for 30-40 minutes then brush with heated apricot glaze.

Salad of Mediterranean vegetables with char grilled scallops

serves 4

12 shelled, hand dived or king scallops

1 x 20g jar Avruga caviar

6 baby aubergines

2 courgettes

1 red pepper

1 yellow pepper

1 green pepper

8 marinated baby artichokes,
cut in half

2 cloves garlic

1 leek, cut into julienne strips
and deep-fried

$^1/_2$ bunch chives, cut into 1" strips

2 sprigs of thyme

small bag seasonal leaves

for the basil oil

100ml virgin olive oil

50ml grapeseed oil

1 bunch of basil

for the marinade

50ml balsamic vinegar

150ml virgin olive oil

150ml grapeseed oil

2 cloves garlic

8 black peppercorns

2 sprigs thyme

10 sprigs coriander

1 dessertspoon of rock salt

Except for the scallops, everything can be prepared 2 days in advance.

Place all the ingredients for the marinade in a saucepan and leave on a gentle heat for 30 minutes or until it just begins to bubble. Remove and leave to stand for 2-5 hours and allow the oil to infuse with all the flavours.

For the basil oil, pick off the leaves and blanch in boiling water for 10-15 seconds. Refresh in ice-cold water and dry on kitchen paper. Blitz in a blender with the oils for 2-3 minutes and pass through a fine sieve or muslin. (This will keep for 1 week in the fridge.)

Trim the bottoms off the peppers so they can sit upright on a tray, drizzle with oil, place the garlic and the thyme on top and season. Roast in an oven 160°C/Gas Mark 3 for 20-25 minutes or until the skins darken and start to wrinkle. Remove and put into an airtight container so they sweat – making it easier to remove the skin. Place a grill pan on a high heat with a drizzle of oil. In the meantime slice the courgettes into 1" thick slices and cut the baby aubergines in half. Char grill the vegetables on both sides until almost cooked through, put into an airtight container or pickling jar. Skin the peppers and discard the seeds, cut to the required shape and mix with the other vegetables. Strain the marinade over the vegetables and add the strips of chives. Leave in the fridge for 36-48 hours.

To serve, add a splash of olive oil to a hot non-stick pan and add the scallops. Leave on a high heat for 1 minute until the scallops start to form a crust, turn over and season with salt, pepper and lemon juice. Remove from the pan onto a small dish. Arrange the leaves on the bottom of the plates and place the marinated vegetables on top. The oils from the vegetables will dress the leaves on their own. Season with ground pepper and rock salt. Place 3 scallops around the side of the salad and 3 artichoke halves in between. Drizzle the basil oil over the top and garnish with a small pile of deep fried leek.

Loin of lamb wrapped with chicken and tarragon mousse, mint pea risotto and baby winter vegetables with rosemary and redcurrant jus

serves 4

4 racks of English lamb
(ask your butcher to remove the eye of the meat and trim away sinew and fat)

150g pig's caul
(available from the butcher)

500g baby spinach, blanched

for the chicken and tarragon mousse

100g diced, skinless chicken

1 egg yolk

150ml whipping cream

salt and pepper

20g chopped tarragon

for the rosemary and redcurrant jus

500ml good veal stock

500ml good lamb stock

3 tablespoons of red wine

1 tablespoon of port

2 sprigs of rosemary

1 dessertspoon redcurrant jelly

for the garnish

2 bunches baby carrots, blanched

2 bunches baby turnips, blanched

2 bunches baby beetroot, blanched

1 bunch of leeks, blanched

for the risotto

1.2 litre chicken stock

2 shallots, finely chopped

1 clove of garlic, crushed

100g unsalted butter

200g pea purée

225g Arborio rice

75g grated Parmesan

chopped mint to taste

To make the jus, put the stocks in a large pan with the rosemary and reduce by 2/3. Put the jelly, red wine and port into a small pan and simmer until reduced by half. Add the reduced stocks and simmer until reduced to a good coating consistency. Remove from the heat and leave to one side.

For the chicken and tarragon mousse, chill a blender bowl in the freezer for 8-10 minutes. Remove the bowl and add the chicken and salt, mix until smooth. Add the egg yolk and mix until blended in with the chicken and slowly add the cream. Remove from the blender and mix in the chopped tarragon.

Seal the lamb in a hot non-stick frying pan for 20 seconds on each side and season. Lay out a piece of pig's caul 150mm x 200mm. Place the blanched, baby spinach on top and evenly coat 3mm thick with the mousseline. Place the sealed lamb on top of the mousse and wrap, ensuring the pigs caul overlaps by 50mm. Leave in the fridge for 20 minutes to firm.

Sprinkle the grated Parmesan evenly over a non-stick tray. Place in the oven at 180oC/Gas Mark 4 for 5 minutes. Remove from the oven and cut into 4 even triangular shapes, leave to one side.

To make the risotto, melt the butter in a pan, add the shallots and garlic and sweat until softened.

Add the rice and stir for a couple of minutes, until translucent. Gradually add the stock a little at a time (100ml) until the rice is cooked, but remains al dente. Remove from the heat and add the Parmesan, pea purée and mint. Check for seasoning and keep warm.

Drizzle olive oil in a hot non-stick pan, seal the lamb again and put in the oven at 180°C/Gas Mark 4 for 12-15 minutes. When cooked to your liking remove from the oven and stand to rest for 5 minutes.

To serve, re-heat all the vegetables in a pan with a little butter and sugar to give them a shine and season to taste. Re-heat the jus. Form a quenelle from the risotto using 2 evenly sized spoons. Place on the plate with a Parmesan tuile (optional). Top and tail the lamb and cut at an angle of 45 degrees, place next to the risotto, share out the glazed baby vegetables and spoon jus around the plate.

Chocolate and pistachio millefeuille with blood orange sorbet

serves 8

for the chocolate mousse

90g milk chocolate

90g whipping cream

30g water

1 leaf gelatine

Melt the milk chocolate, dissolve the gelatine in water and add to the chocolate and fold in the whipped cream.

for the pistachio butter cream

125g sugar

1 egg yolk

1 egg

190g butter

2 teaspoons dark pistachio paste (available from a good delicatessen)

To make the sabayon/butter cream, melt the sugar to softball 121˚C. Mix the egg with the yolk and add the sugar with a little water. Mix until cooler then add knobs of butter and pistachio paste.

for the pistachio biscuit

100g butter

40g sugar

130g soft flour

20g pistachio nuts, finely chopped

Cream the butter and sugar, add the flour and pistachio nuts and place in the fridge for 20 minutes. Then roll into rectangles and lightly bake.

for the blood orange sorbet

500g blood orange purée

125g stock syrup

Juice of 1 lemon

Place purée, syrup and lemon juice in a pan and boil. Cool and place in an ice cream machine and churn. Once frozen, quenelle with 2 dessertspoons.

for the orange caramel syrup

150g sugar

75g orange juice

Make a direct caramel with the sugar, then add the orange juice and reduce down to syrup.

for the biscuit tuile garnish

50g egg white (1 1/2 egg whites)

55g flour

55g icing sugar

35g melted butter

Mix the egg white, icing sugar and flour, then the melted butter. Chill thoroughly. Pipe small lines on a non-stick mat and cook until brown. Wrap round something circular to shape.

To make the chocolate shapes, temper some dark chocolate to 32˚C and white chocolate to 28˚C. Spread dark chocolate on an acetate sheet and 'wood-grain' it with a stencil. Leave to set and spread with white chocolate. When nearly set, cut out rectangles and place in the fridge to firm up with a weight on top to keep flat.

To serve, place 1 rectangle of chocolate on the plate, pipe milk chocolate mousse on the chocolate, then add the rectangle of pistachio biscuit. Pipe the pistachio butter cream onto the biscuit and place another chocolate rectangle on top to finish the millefeuille. Place the tuile garnish on one edge of the dessert so it stands up and place 3 orange segments on the plate with the orange caramel sauce. Finish with a quenelle of blood orange sorbet and a spring of mint.

THE GRAND HOTEL

Keith Mitchell

Salmon and turbot parcel with nori seaweed, asparagus and mussel sauce with saffron

serves 4

300g Scottish salmon fillet, skinned

200g turbot fillet, skinned

4 sheets of nori seaweed

250g new potatoes

75g butter

2 teaspoons chopped fresh dill

16 asparagus spears

salt and freshly ground black pepper

For the mussel sauce

400g mussels, well scrubbed
(discard any open ones that won't
close when pressed lightly)

150ml dry white wine

200ml double cream

a pinch of saffron

Keeping the knife flat, cut the salmon fillet in half lengthways to produce 2 thin fillets. Sandwich the turbot between the salmon fillets and cut into 4 equal portions. Wrap each one in a sheet of nori, trimming off any excess and tucking in the ends. Then wrap in clingfilm so it is completely enclosed. When required, steam in the clingfilm for 8 minutes, then leave to rest in a warm place for 4-5 minutes.

Meanwhile, heat a large dry saucepan until very hot, add the mussels, then the wine and immediately cover tightly with a lid or foil. Cook for about 1 minute on full heat, until the mussels open, then take off the heat and strain, reserving the cooking liquid. Remove the mussels from their shells and set aside.

Strain the mussel cooking liquor through a cloth into a clean pan and simmer until reduced by half. Add the cream and saffron and simmer until reduced to a light coating consistency.

Cook the new potatoes in boiling salted water until tender, then drain. Lightly crush with 50g of the butter and the dill and season to taste.

Cook the asparagus in boiling salted water, then drain and toss with the remaining butter and some seasoning.

Gently reheat the mussels in the sauce for 30 seconds.

To serve, cut the fish in half at an angle with the clingfilm still on, then discard the clingfilm. Divide the crushed potatoes between 4 large serving plates and place the fish on top, then arrange the asparagus on one side and the mussels and sauce on the other.

Fillet of lamb with chicken and wild mushroom mousseline, creamed garlic potato, savoy cabbage and a redcurrant jus

serves 4

2 racks of English lamb (ask your butcher to remove the 'eye' of the meat in one piece, trimming away any sinew and fat)

100g caul fat

400g large carrots

a pinch of sugar

a knob of butter

400g old potatoes, cut into chunks

4 garlic cloves, sliced

50ml double cream

2 tablespoons vegetable oil

salt and freshly ground black pepper

For the redcurrant jus

1.5 litres good lamb stock

1 dessertspoon redcurrant jelly

4 tablespoons red wine

For the mousseline

100g skinless boneless chicken breast, diced

a good pinch of salt

1/2 egg white

150ml double cream

100g girolles (or other wild mushrooms), cleaned and roughly chopped

For the cabbage

100g smoked back bacon, cut into fine strips

a knob of butter

400g Savoy cabbage, shredded and blanched

To make the redcurrant jus, put the stock in a large, wide pan and boil until reduced to about 200ml. Put the redcurrant jelly and wine in a small pan and stir over a low heat until the jelly has melted, then simmer until reduced and sticky. Add the reduced lamb stock and simmer until reduced to a good coating consistency. Remove from the heat and set aside.

For the mousseline, place the chicken in a food processor bowl, then chill it in the freezer with the bowl and blade for 10 minutes. Remove from the freezer, add the salt and process to a smooth paste. Add the egg white and blend until incorporated, then gradually blend in the cream. Fold in the wild mushrooms by hand. Spoon the mousseline on to the lamb fillets and wrap each one in the caul fat, with a 5cm overlap underneath. Set aside in a cool place.

Slice the carrots lengthways and cut them into petal shapes. Cook in a minimum of salted water with a good pinch of sugar and a knob of butter, until the carrots are tender and the liquid has evaporated.

Meanwhile, cook the potatoes with the garlic in boiling salted water until tender. Drain well, push through a sieve or a potato ricer and mix in the cream. Season to taste and keep warm.

For the cabbage, fry the bacon gently in the butter, then add the blanched cabbage, cover and cook gently until tender. Keep warm.

Heat the vegetable oil in a large ovenproof frying pan, add the lamb fillets and seal in the hot oil for 2 minutes, turning carefully, to give a little colour. Transfer to an oven preheated to 160°C/Gas Mark 3 and cook for 12 minutes, then leave to rest in a warm place for 5 minutes. Reheat the sauce if necessary.

To assemble the dish, divide the potato between 4 serving plates and arrange the carrots around the edge. Put the cabbage and bacon next to the carrots. Slice the lamb and arrange on top of the cabbage, then pour the sauce around.

Chocolate and mascarpone cream délice with griottine cherries

serves 4

150g good-quality plain chocolate

30g caster sugar

250g mascarpone cheese

250ml double cream, lightly whipped

150ml good-quality white chocolate

200g jar of Griottine cherries in kirsch or brandy

1 heaped teaspoon arrowroot

cocoa powder for dusting

For the biscuit base

75g unsalted butter

75g soft brown sugar

50g plain flour

1/2 teaspoon bicarbonate of soda

a pinch of salt

50g rolled oats

For the biscuit base, put all the ingredients except the oats in an electric mixer and beat until smooth. Stir in the oats. Roll out the mixture between 2 sheets of baking parchment until 2-3mm thick. Remove the top sheet of paper, slide the mixture on the bottom sheet on to a flat baking tray and bake in an oven preheated to 200°C/Gas Mark 6 for 7-8 minutes, until golden brown. While it is still warm, cut out 4 rounds with a plain 6.5cm cutter.

Melt the plain chocolate and half the sugar in a bowl set over a pan of barely simmering water, making sure the water isn't touching the base of the bowl. Remove from the heat and stir in half the mascarpone while the chocolate is still warm, then fold in half the whipped cream. In a separate bowl, repeat with the white chocolate and the remaining sugar, mascarpone and cream.

Place the biscuit rounds in the base of four 6.5cm cutters or ring moulds and line the sides with a 6.5cm-high strip of baking parchment. Half fill each one with the dark chocolate mixture.

Drain the cherries and reserve the liquor. Cut some of the cherries in half and place a ring of cherry halves on top of the dark chocolate mixture, with the cut surfaces against the lined mould. Top up the moulds with the white chocolate mixture, smooth the top and chill until set.

Return the remaining cherries to the liquor and bring to a simmer. Mix the arrowroot to a paste with a little water, then stir this mixture into the liquor and simmer for a minute or two, until slightly thickened. Leave to cool.

Dust the top of each délice with cocoa powder and remove the rings. Place on 4 serving plates, peel off the paper and allow to return to room temperature for about 20 minutes. Spoon the cherries and their liquor on to the plates and serve.

CHARLTON HOUSE
AND THE MULBERRY RESTAURANT
Adam Fellows

Fillet of red mullet with new potatoes, herb salad and red wine and caper vinaigrette

serves 4

4 red mullet, approx 300g each

16 new potatoes

mixed salad and herb leaves

4 tablespoons Cabernet Sauvignon red wine vinegar

4 tablespoons olive oil

4 teaspoons fine capers

1 tablespoon chopped flat parsley

2 spring onions

2 slices of pancetta

1 small shallot, chopped

Fillet the red mullet, remove all the bones and rinse under cold water. Place on a tray with olive oil and reserve.

Cook and peel the new potatoes and cut into 1cm slices. Sauté in a frying pan until golden. Cut the pancetta into small strips (lardons) and add to the pan with the potatoes. Continue to cook until coloured. Chop the spring onion and also add to the pan, continue to cook for 1 further minute. Season and then place on to kitchen paper to dry.

Reduce the red wine vinegar with the shallot by half. Whisk in the olive oil then add the capers and chopped parsley. Cook the red mullet under the grill for 5-6 minutes.

To serve, place the potatoes on the base of the plate. Put the red mullet on top of them and pour the vinaigrette around. Finish with the mixed lettuce and herb leaves. Pour over a little dressing.

Poached wood pigeon with a lentil and foie gras broth

serves 4

4 wood pigeons

4 slices of foie gras

100g puy lentils, pre-soaked

1 shallot

1 clove of garlic

1 tablespoon each of chopped carrot, celery, and leek

1/3 litre chicken stock

10g pancetta

1 sprig of thyme

8 cabbage leaves

150g small girolles

100g celeriac

20g flat parsley, chopped

for the chicken mousse

1 chicken breast

1 egg

150ml cream

salt and pepper

You will only need about 50g of mousse, but it is difficult to make any less. Blend the chicken meat until smooth and add the egg, salt and pepper. In a bowl, gently incorporate the cream and check the seasoning.

Remove the breasts from the bone of the pigeon. Blanch the cabbage leaves and pat dry with kitchen paper. Lay out 2 leaves of cabbage on a piece of cling film. Spread with a little chicken mousse and place the breast on top. Wrap around the leaves and then roll into a sausage shape with the cling film. Poach at 85°C for 5 minutes and leave to rest for 5 minutes.

Sweat all the chopped vegetables with the garlic, thyme and pancetta in a saucepan. Add the lentils and stock and cook until soft. Blend with a hand blender adding a little butter and seasoning, to create the lentil broth.

Cut celeriac into a dice and blanch in boiling salted water. Sauté the girolles in a hot frying pan and when coloured add the celeriac dice and finish with chopped parsley.

Place the broth in a bowl, add the pigeon cut in half and place a slice of pan-fried foie gras on the top. Spoon the girolles and celeriac dice around the outside of the pigeon.

Apple and vanilla parfait, blackcurrant sorbet

serves 4

5 apples, peeled and cubed

juice of 1 lemon

1 vanilla pod

100g sugar

2 egg yolks

1 cup caster sugar

double measure of calvados

500ml whipping cream,
lightly whipped

150g egg whites

For the vanilla syrup

200g caster sugar

100ml water

20g glucose

1 split vanilla pod

for the blackcurrant sorbet

1 litre blackcurrant coulis

300ml stock syrup
(available from good supermarkets)

small scoop of glucose

juice of 1 lemon

Make a compôte by placing the apple, vanilla and lemon in a saucepan and cook until soft. Remove from the heat and leave to cool.

To make the sabayon, take a bowl and whisk the egg yolks and a cup of sugar, cook over a pan of water for 7-8 minutes until thick. Remove from the heat and leave to cool.

For the parfait, whisk the egg whites in a bowl until stiff. Add the remaining sugar and continue to whisk for 1 minute. Mix three-quarters of the apple compôte with the sabayon and fold in the meringue, (the remaining compôte will be used to serve). Then fold in the lightly whipped cream and calvados. Spoon into ring moulds, smooth level and freeze.

To make the vanilla syrup, place everything into a saucepan and bring to the boil. Remove from the heat, leave to cool and transfer into a squirty bottle, if you have one, otherwise a spoon will do.

To make the blackcurrant sorbet, boil all the ingredients, apart from the coulis (which can either be made or bought in packets or jars) and whisk, leave to cool. Churn in an ice-cream machine and place in the freezer.

To serve, place the parfait on to the left hand side of the plate and using two teaspoons, make a quenelle of apple compôte and place on to the parfait. Spoon the sorbet to the right hand side and squirt or spoon the vanilla syrup over and around the parfait. Garnish with a little mint and pieces of dried vanilla.

STUDLEY PRIORY

Simon Crannage

Seared scallops, herb risotto

serves 4

12 fresh scallops

4 small cups lined with blanched spinach

12 cherry tomatoes

1 aubergine skin,
cut into fine strips and deep-fried

340g cooked risotto rice

chopped mint leaves

pinch of grated Parmesan

olive oil for cooking

First, brush 4 demitasse cups with melted butter and season, then line with sheets of blanched spinach. Start to warm a pan for the scallops.

In a saucepan, add some olive oil and the cooked risotto rice. When warm, add the Parmesan and season to taste, then add the chopped herbs and some more olive oil to moisten. Keep warm.

Salt the tops of the scallops and place them salt-side down in the pre-heated pan, cook until golden.

To serve, fill the cups with the rice mixture and turn out onto the plate. Place 3 scallops on top with some warmed cherry tomatoes. Garnish with crisp aubergine skin.

Roast squab pigeon, Grenadine sauce, cabbage parcel and wild mushrooms

serves 4

4 oven ready squab pigeons

for the sauce

600 ml good strong veal stock
(or chicken)

shallots

sprig thyme

20ml Grenadine

for the cabbage parcel

blanched green cabbage leaves

yellow cabbage, cut into strips

2 diced carrots

$^1/_2$ diced celeriac

2 diced shallots

for the vegetables

*Savoy cabbage,
green split from the yellow leaves*

6 Morel mushrooms

Pleurotte mushrooms

baby carrots, turnips, leeks per portion

To make the cabbage parcel, add a small amount of butter to a large pan and sauté the carrot, shallot and celeriac until soft. Then add the yellow strips of the cabbage and stir until limp. Line a ladle with the blanched green leaves and fill with the cabbage mixture. Wrap this ball in cling film and shape.

Salt the inside of the squab pigeons. Heat a heavy-bottomed, ovenproof dish with a little vegetable oil, until very hot. Place the birds, skin-side down, in the dish and cook until golden. Then turn to the over side. Place in oven at 190°C/Gas Mark 5.

For the Grenadine sauce, heat a saucepan with a little butter. Add the shallots and thyme. When soft add the Grenadine and reduce by half. Add the veal stock and reduce to a nice coating consistency. Keep warm.

Sauté the mushrooms in a little oil and season. Warm the baby vegetables and season.

To serve, arrange the mushrooms and vegetables rustically around a large pasta bowl. Plunge the cabbage ball into boiling water to heat, then remove the cling film. Place the ball in the middle of the bowl. Take the squab out of the oven and place on top of the cabbage (the breasts can easily be taken off the bone at this stage). Finish by bringing the sauce back to the boil and pouring over the vegetable garnish.

Miniature summer desserts

serves 4

Raspberry and red wine jelly

1 punnet raspberries

500ml Cabernet Sauvignon

50g caster sugar

4 leaves of gelatine

1 vanilla pod
split in half and scraped

the zest of 1 lemon

Bring the wine to the boil, add the sugar, zest of lemon and vanilla pod. Remove from heat and allow to cool.

Meanwhile soak the gelatine in a little cold water to soften, then dissolve in warm red wine mixture.

Rinse the raspberries and pat dry with kitchen paper. Pass the wine mixture through a fine sieve. Àrrange raspberries in the bottom of desired moulds (brioche moulds were used in this instance), cover with wine mixture and refrigerate overnight.

Blueberry blancmange

450ml double cream

50ml blueberry purée

1 punnet raspberries

3 leaves of gelatine

50g caster sugar

1 vanilla pod

Soak the gelatine leaves in cold water. Cut the vanilla pod in half and scrape seeds into the cream. Add caster sugar and stir to the boil using a wooden spoon, then incorporate the softened gelatine. Remove from the heat and add the blueberry purée.

Cool this mixture for 5-10 minutes before adding the blueberries and pouring into moulds and refrigerate overnight.

To serve, dip the mould into hot water for a couple of seconds and turn onto plate. Garnish with spun caramel.

WATERFORD CASTLE

Michael Quinn

Oyster and scallop feuillantine with crisp leeks and tomato beurre blanc

serves 4

4 round slices of aubergine

4 tablespoons mushroom soy

4 tablespoons balsamic vinegar

1 garlic clove, cut into slivers

4 sprigs of thyme

2 large sheets of filo pastry

1 egg white, lightly beaten

1/2 leek

oil for deep-frying

olive oil

16 fresh scallops

16 fresh oysters

a knob of butter

salt and freshly ground white pepper

For the tomato beurre blanc

25g shallot or onion, finely chopped

1 tablespoon white wine vinegar

1 tablespoon dry white wine

50ml double cream

150g chilled unsalted butter, cut into small cubes

1 ripe tomato, skinned, deseeded and cut into 5mm cubes

Marinate the aubergine slices in the mushroom soy, balsamic vinegar, garlic and thyme for 15 minutes. Meanwhile, make the sauce. Put the shallot or onion, vinegar and wine into a small saucepan and simmer until only 1 tablespoon of liquid is left. Add the cream and simmer until reduced by half. Take the pan off the heat and gradually whisk in the pieces of butter, a few at a time, until you have a light emulsion. Keep warm.

Grill the marinated aubergine for 3 minutes on each side, until tender. Set aside.

Lay out one sheet of filo pastry on a clean work surface and brush with egg white. Place the second sheet of filo on top and brush with egg white again. Leave to dry for a few minutes and then cut into 12 circles about 7cm in diameter. Place the circles on a baking tray and cover with baking parchment to prevent the pastry rising. Bake in an oven preheated to 180°C/Gas Mark 4 for 3 minutes or until golden.

Slice the leek lengthways, separate the layers and continue to slice lengthways as thinly as possible. Deep-fry for a few minutes, until crisp, then drain on kitchen paper and set aside.

Heat a little olive oil in a large frying pan until very hot. Season the scallops and sauté them for 2 minutes, until golden brown underneath, then turn over and cook for 1 minute longer. At the last moment add the oysters and a small knob of butter to the pan. Cook for 30 seconds and remove from the heat.

To serve, place a slice of grilled aubergine in the centre of each plate, followed by a filo disc, then top with 2 oysters and 2 scallops, followed by a filo disc. Follow with the remaining oysters and scallops then the third filo disc and place the crisp leeks on top. Finally pour the sauce around the plate and garnish it with the tomato.

Fillet of brill with a soft parsley crust, tomato fondue and mussel and mustard velouté

serves 4

3 tablespoons Dijon mustard

1 brill, weighing about 1.2kg, filleted into 4 and skinned

3 tablespoons olive oil

50ml water

2 sprigs of thyme

3 tablespoons double cream

sea salt and freshly ground white pepper

For the parsley crust

220g salted butter

220g soft white breadcrumbs

100g curly-leaf parsley

zest and juice of 1 lemon

For the tomato fondue

1 onion, finely chopped

3 garlic cloves, crushed

3 tablespoons olive oil

16 ripe tomatoes, skinned, deseeded and finely chopped

3 tablespoons raspberry vinegar

3 tablespoons roughly chopped fresh tarragon

For the mussels

20 mussels, well scrubbed (discard any open ones that won't close when pressed lightly)

1 shallot, diced

1/2 garlic clove, crushed

1/2 glass of white wine

Make the parsley crust by blending the butter and breadcrumbs together in a food processor, then adding the parsley, lemon zest and juice and blending until vibrant green. Line a chopping board with clingfilm and pour the mixture on to it. Cover with more clingfilm and roll out with a rolling pin until it is 1cm thick. Place the crust in the fridge for a few hours until it firms up, then cut it into 4 pieces about the same size as the fish fillets.

For the tomato fondue, sweat the onion and garlic in the olive oil for 3 minutes, then add the tomatoes and raspberry vinegar and cook for 15 minutes on a low heat, until reduced and thickened. Add the tarragon and season to taste, then set aside.

Put all the ingredients for the mussels in a large pan, cover and cook over a high heat for a few minutes, until the mussels have opened; discard any that remain closed. Drain the mussels and keep warm.

Spread 2 tablespoons of the Dijon mustard over the fish fillets and place the parsley crust cut-outs over the fish. Place carefully in a shallow baking dish, crust-side up. Pour the olive oil, water and the sprigs of thyme around the fish, being careful not to wet the crust. Bake in an oven preheated to 200°C/Gas Mark 6 for 5-8 minutes, until the fish is just done. Using a palette knife, lift the fish out and keep warm.

Boil the cooking liquid for 1 minute and then stir in the remaining mustard and the cream. Taste and adjust the seasoning. Reheat the tomato fondue if necessary and divide it between 4 plates. Place the fish on top, pour the sauce around and add the cooked mussels.

Blackberry and apple crumble tarts with ginger ice-cream

serves 4

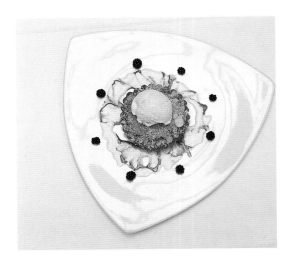

6 dessert apples, peeled, cored and cut into slices 1cm thick

180g caster sugar

juice of 1 lemon

40g blackberries

For the ginger ice cream

250ml milk

250ml double cream

1 teaspoon finely grated fresh root ginger

1 vanilla pod, split open lengthways

5 egg yolks

60g caster sugar

For the pastry

200g plain flour

75g icing sugar

25g ground almonds

120g unsalted butter, diced

1 egg, beaten

For the crumble

115g plain flour

40g ground almonds

40g caster sugar

85g unsalted butter, diced

20g flaked almonds, toasted

First make the ice-cream. Put the milk and cream in a saucepan, add the ginger and vanilla pod and bring to a simmer. Whisk the egg yolks and sugar together in a large bowl and pour the milk and cream mixture on to them, stirring all the time. Return to the saucepan and cook over a low heat, stirring constantly, until the mixture is thick enough to coat the back of the spoon (do not let it boil). Remove the vanilla pod and leave to cool, then freeze in an ice-cream machine.

To make the pastry, sift the flour and icing sugar into a bowl and stir in the ground almonds. Rub in the butter until the mixture resembles breadcrumbs, then make a well in the centre and pour in the egg. Stir together to make a dough and then knead very lightly until smooth. Wrap in clingfilm and leave to rest in the fridge for 30 minutes.

Divide the pastry into 4 and roll each piece out on a lightly floured surface. Use to line 4 greased 7.5cm flan tins, gently easing the dough into the corners. Chill again for 30 minutes, then line with greaseproof paper, fill with enough baking beans to ensure that the sides are

supported and bake in an oven preheated to 180°C/Gas Mark 4 for 8 minutes. Remove the beans and paper and return to the oven for 5 minutes.

For the crumble, mix the flour, ground almonds and sugar together in a bowl and rub in the butter until the mixture resembles breadcrumbs. Knead the mixture together, wrap it in clingfilm and leave to rest in the fridge for 30 minutes. Roll it out on lightly floured greaseproof paper until it is 5mm thick. Place on a baking tray and bake in an oven preheated to 180°C/Gas Mark 4 for 15 minutes, until golden brown. Leave to cool, then crumble it with your fingers to a breadcrumb texture. Mix in the toasted almonds.

To make the filling, put the apple slices in a saucepan with the sugar and lemon juice. Cook, covered, over a low heat until soft. Remove from the heat and stir in the blackberries. Divide the warm filling between the flan cases and cover each one generously with the crumble mixture. Place each tart in the centre of a serving plate and top with a ball of the ginger ice-cream.

THATCHED COTTAGE HOTEL & RESTAURANT

Martin Matysik

New Forest wild mushrooms with tarragon flavoured organic carrots

serves 4

a selection of 8-12 varieties of New Forest or other wild mushrooms

1 garlic clove, finely chopped

2 shallots, finely chopped

2 tablespoons of sherry

2 tablespoons of veal stock

25g clarified butter

25g tarragon

Clean the mushrooms and cut into equal pieces. In a sauté pan, simmer olive oil with garlic, shallots and mushrooms. Deglaze with sherry. Add the veal stock and continue to simmer for 5 minutes until the mushrooms are tender. Before serving with the tarragon carrots, sprinkle the mushrooms with a little lemon juice - this will help lift each mushroom's natural flavour.

Cut the carrots into ribbons using a potato peeler and steam 'al dente' for 2-3 minutes. Melt the clarified butter in a pan adding the tarragon, remove the carrots and place in the flavoured butter before serving.

The wild duckling symphony duet

The supreme à l'orange with potato crêpes and cocoa glazed baby turnips, followed by its leglet with foie gras and a confit of black and white grapes

serves 4

*2 whole wild ducklings
hung for 21 days*

12 baby turnips

for the orange consommé

juice of 4 oranges

100g caster sugar

Bring to the boil and reduce over a low heat to concentrate.

for the duck sauce

50g sugar

2 tablespoons red wine vinegar

200ml veal stock

50ml orange consomme

roasted duck wings

10g butter

for the potato crêpes

200g potato purée

50g sifted flour

2 beaten eggs

pinch of salt and grated nutmeg

50ml milk

for the grape confit

200g peeled whole red grapes

100ml port wine

25g butter

Season the duckling with salt and pepper. Sauté to brown both sides of the breasts, then place in the oven 200°C/Gas Mark 6 for 10 minutes, reduce the heat to 130°C/Gas Mark 1 to rest the meat for a further 10 minutes. Remove the wings for the sauce.

For the duck sauce, caramelise the sugar in a heavy saucepan, deglazing with red wine vinegar. Reduce to a syrup, add the veal stock, orange consomme and the reserved duck winglets. Reduce by half. Season with salt and pepper and sieve, return to a clean pan and add cold butter flakes to thicken.

To make the potato crêpes, place the potato purée, flour, beaten eggs and seasoning in a blender, gradually add the milk until the pancake mixture is smooth. In a lightly buttered pancake pan over a low heat, cook 3 baby pancakes for each person until golden brown. Set aside and keep warm.

Trim the excess greens from the turnips and halve. Cook for 8-10 minutes in simmering water until tender. Remove and season with butter flakes, salt and pepper. Place the turnips on the plate and sprinkle with a mixture of cocoa powder and caster sugar, place under a very hot grill to caramelise.

To serve the first part of the main course, remove the plate with turnips from the heat. Place the crêpes with orange segments on the plate and drizzle with orange consommé. Slice the duck breasts from the carcass (placing the carcass with leg, back in the oven to finish cooking 190°C/Gas Mark 5, for 10 minutes). Slice the breasts and place on the plate, cover with the duck sauce which has a little cream added, to give a marble effect.

For the consecutive main course, reduce the heat to 130°C/Gas Mark 1 to rest the leg meat.

For the black and white grape confit, caramelise the sugar in a saucepan, adding the port wine and reducing to a syrup. Stir in the butter and add the peeled grapes. Meanwhile briefly sauté each person a generous portion of foie gras, seasoning it with salt and pepper.

To serve, place on the plate together with a spoon of grape confit and roasted leglet of wild duckling.

Drunken strawberry soufflé with mint flavoured white chocolate sauce

serves 4

1kg strawberries

500ml quality Kirsch Schnapps

100ml almond flavoured sugar syrup

Wash and trim handpicked organic strawberries and place in the Kirsch marinade 2-6 days before use.

for the soufflé

400g Kirsch marinated strawberries

8 egg whites

3 tablespoons of caster sugar

20g butter

for the white chocolate sauce

200g grated white chocolate

100ml milk

100ml double cream

50ml mint syrup

Grease 4 soufflé dishes and sprinkle with caster sugar making sure you cover the bottom and sides and refrigerate. In a bowl, beat the egg whites to soft peaks. Using a slotted spoon, add the marinated strawberries. Continue to whisk for 1 minute or stop when the strawberries are bruised and blended.

Scoop out the mixture into the prepared soufflé dishes, wiping around the rims for a neat finish. Bake in an oven at 180°C/Gas Mark 4, for 10 minutes. While the soufflé cooks and rises prepare the white chocolate sauce.

Put all the sauce ingredients into a saucepan and bring slowly to the boil, stirring with a wooden spoon until amalgamated. Pour into a sauce bowl and serve with the risen soufflé.

Variations on flavoured soufflés often featured on our menus:

Banana and lime soufflé with bitter chocolate rum sauce

Follow the above recipe substituting 2 ripe bananas and zest of 1 lime to blend in with the egg white. For the sauce, substitute with dark bitter chocolate and a good shot of golden rum.

Passion fruit soufflé with avocado sauce

Follow the above recipe substituting the pulp of 8 ripe passion fruits to mix with the egg whites. Also utilising 2 ripe avocados, 200ml milk, and 2 tablespoons clear honey - just briefly boil together and blend.

Pear soufflé - 'Belle Helene' with chocolate coated vanilla ice cream

Use pre-poached Williams's pears to mix into the egg whites, adding pear Williams Schnapps. The vanilla bean ice cream is dipped in melted milk chocolate and sprinkled with toasted almond flakes.

WOOD NORTON HALL

Steve Waites

Assiette of seafood

serves 4

75g fillet of sea bass

for the spring rolls

2 spring roll papers

2 cooked oysters, quartered

2 cooked mussels, quartered

25g of white crab meat

2 cooked scallops, quartered

1 egg

sprig of coriander, finely sliced

knob of butter

1/2 shallot

1/2 of a whole chilli, chopped

1 teaspoon chopped chives

a little lemon juice

for the tian

4 plum tomatoes

1/2 ripe avocado

100g prawns

1 tablespoon mayonnaise

juice of 1/2 lemon

for the niçoise salad

75g loin of raw tuna

potato purée

1 egg white

5 chives

4 fine green beans,
cooked and cut into quarters

mixed lettuce
(rocket, mizuna, baby spinach)

4 black olives pitted and cut into quarters

to garnish

fresh basil leaves

tomato coulis

Start by making the spring rolls. Take the scallops, mussels, oysters and crab meat and add the finely chopped shallots, chives and chillies and coriander. Bind the ingredients together with a little softened butter. Add a little lemon juice and seasoning to taste. Place the filling in the middle of the spring roll papers and roll, sealing the edges with egg wash. Bake in the oven an approximately 180°C/Gas Mark 4 until golden brown. Cut each roll in half lengthways and place one on each plate.

For the tian, blanch the plum tomatoes, skin and deseed. Cut in half and cut 2 round shapes from each tomato. Dice the avocado, season and add a squeeze of lemon juice. Chop up the prawns and mix with the lemon juice and mayonnaise. Neatly place a tomato diamond on a plate, layer with prawn and avocado mixtures and top with the second tomato diamond.

Salt the sea bass 10 minutes before cooking, then sear in a hot thick-bottomed pan with a little melted butter for approximately 3 minutes and divide into 4.

For the niçoise salad, thinly slice the raw tuna fillet and season. Next make the potato wavers by mixing the potato purée with the egg white, chives and seasoning. Spread evenly and cook on silicone paper in a medium oven until golden brown. To assemble the salad, layer the green beans, potato wavers, tuna, lettuce and olives.

To serve, place the items on a plate and garnish with the fresh basil leaves and tomato coulis.

Sauté of pork, confit of belly, boulangère potatoes with creamed parsnip

serves 4

4 x 150g mignons pork
(small and tender cuts of meat)

knob of unsalted butter

a little olive oil

4 sprigs of rosemary

8 sage leaves, deep-fried

for the pork confit of belly

250g rock salt

1kg pork belly

1 sprig rosemary, chopped

1 sprig thyme, chopped

1 sprig sage, chopped

1kg duck fat

2 cloves garlic, split

1 metre of muslin cloth

for the sauce

1kg pork bones

3 litres dark pork stock

1 peeled banana shallot

2 peeled sticks of celery

1 peeled carrot

1 leek

1 green dessert apple

1 measure of Calvados

50g tomato paste

for the creamed parsnip

250g parsnips, peeled

250g potatoes, peeled

250ml milk

250ml double cream

knob of butter

for the boulangère potatoes

1 banana shallot,
peeled and sliced into roundelles

4 white potatoes cut into cylinders

250ml chicken stock

2 carrots, peeled

knob of butter

24 hours before cooking, mix the rosemary and sage with the salt and rub onto the pork belly and refrigerate. The following day, wash off the salt and herbs and pat dry, then place between double thickness of muslin cloth and roll tightly until it resembles a sausage shape. Tie the ends and put into an ovenproof dish. Cover with the duck fat and add the garlic and the thyme. Cover and place in the oven for 3 hours, at 180°C/Gas Mark 4. Once cooked, take from the oven, remove from the fat and cool. When cold, remove the muslin and cut into 4 slices approximately 2" thick.

For the sauté of pork, take a hot pan and add the butter and oil and lightly fry the seasoned mignons on both sides to seal. Add the confit of pork belly and place in the oven for approximately 8 minutes at 180°C/Gas Mark 4 until the mignons are cooked through.

For the creamed parsnips, slice the parsnips and potatoes and simmer in the milk until soft. Purée with a hand blender, then whisk in a dash of cream and a knob of butter, season to taste.

For the boulangère potatoes, slice the potatoes and carrots and layer into 4 small moulds with the shallots. Pour over the chicken stock and add a little salt. Brush the top with the butter and cook in the oven for approximately 20 minutes at 180°C/Gas Mark 4 until golden brown. Press down when cooked and turn out.

To make the sauce, roast the bones in the oven until golden brown. In a saucepan, sauté the vegetables and apple then add the roasted bones. Add the tomato paste and Calvados and flambé. Pour over the pork stock and simmer for 3 hours. Pass through a muslin cloth and chill. Once cold remove any excess fat.

To serve, reheat the sauce. Place the boulangère potatoes on the plates and place the pork mignons on top. Place the belly confit around the potatoes, together with the creamed parsnips and garnish with the sauce, rosemary sprigs and sage leaves.

Raspberry sorbet tuille with vanilla parfait

serves 4

for the tuille

100g plain flour

100g icing sugar

105g egg whites

100g butter

for the sorbet

1/2 lemon

1/2 orange

1/2 star anise

200g caster sugar

1 vanilla pod

1/2 cinnamon stick

250ml of water

250ml of raspberry purée

for the vanilla parfait

seeds of 4 vanilla pods

750ml of double cream

150g caster sugar

5 egg yolks

2 whole eggs

to garnish

raspberry coulis

fresh raspberries

To make the tuille cones, cream the sugar and butter, then add the flour and egg whites. Chill in the fridge for at least 30 minutes. Once chilled, spread the mixture with a palette knife onto silicone paper into semi circle shapes. Bake in a medium oven until golden. Remove from the paper whilst still warm and shape into cones.

Place the lemon, orange, star anise, sugar, vanilla pod and cinnamon sticks in the water and warm to boiling point. Cool slightly, then strain and add to the raspberry purée; chill and churn to sorbet.

To make the parfait, heat up the sugar in the oven at 160°C/Gas Mark 2½ for approximately 5 minutes. Lightly mix the egg yolks with the whole eggs with a whisk, then add the warm sugar to make a sabayon. Continue to whisk until cold, add the vanilla pod seeds. Whip the cream until thick but not stiff. Fold the whipped cream into the sabayon. Pour into a small terrine mould and set in the freezer.

To serve, press the sorbet into the cones and serve with a slice of the vanilla parfait. Garnish with fresh raspberries and raspberry coulis.

THE OLD BELL AT MALMESBURY

Michael Benjamin

Marinated cockles and clams with basil, served with puréed avocado, carrot and cauliflower

serves 4

250g fresh clams

250g fresh cockles

4 large shallots

olive oil

basil leaves

for the cauliflower

1 tightly closed head of cauliflower

lemon juice

290ml of chicken stock

$^1/_2$ bay leaf

500g carrots

1 ripe avocado

a little crème fraîche

Bring a pan of water to the boil and add the cockles and clams, cook until the shells are open. Refresh under cold running water and remove from their shells. Finely chop the shallots and mix in with the clams and cockles with a small amount of olive oil. At the last minute, add some chopped basil leaves.

Remove the stalks and heart from the cauliflower and roughly chop. Place into a pan with a dash of olive oil, lemon juice and half bay leaf. Just cover with chicken stock and cook until tender. Remove bay leaf and excess water. Blend in a processor into a fine purée and reserve for later use. Repeat the same process for the carrot purée. Take the avocado, peel and blend with a little crème fraîche in a processor until smooth.

To serve, take a cocktail glass, first place the avocado purée in the bottom, then build with marinated cockles and clams, carrot purée and finally, the cauliflower purée. Fill to the rim and smooth over. For a special occasion, replace the cockles and clams with Sevruga caviar.

Roasted 'red legged' partridge with Savoy cabbage, bacon, braised chestnuts and black trumpet mushrooms, served with a white grape sauce

serves 4

1 fresh 'red legged' partridge - available from a game dealer

1 carrot

1 stick of celery

trimmings from the partridge

290ml of brown stock

butter

cream

2 handfuls of seedless white grapes

1 piece of smoked bacon

1 Savoy cabbage

150ml of double cream

24 chestnuts

50g black trumpet mushrooms or small flat cap mushrooms

Ask the butcher to prepare the bird for roasting and keep all the trimmings. Pre-heat the oven to 230°C/Gas Mark 8, and place the bird in a pan with oil and butter and cook for 9 minutes, basting well with the fat. Remove from the oven and allow to rest. Remove the legs and place back in the oven for a further 2 minutes.

To make the sauce, add a small amount of butter to the pan in which the bird was cooked, along with all the trimmings and a little chopped carrot and celery. Cook until lightly coloured and then add the brown stock and a dash of cream. Cook down by half and pass through a fine sieve. At the last minute, add the halved seedless white grapes.

Cut the bacon into 1cm pieces and cook in boiling water. Chop the green leaves from the cabbage into 2cm pieces and cook in the double cream. When the cream has reduced by half, add the bacon.

Take some of the sauce made for the partridge and heat up the chestnuts until they are glazed.

Trim the stalks from the mushrooms and remove any debris and insects. Cook in a small amount of water, butter and seasoning.

Dark 'Valrohna' chocolate torte with cocoa pears and a vanilla bean sauce

serves 4

3 eggs separated

75g stock syrup

160g finest quality dark chocolate

150ml lightly whipped double cream

for the sauce

290ml milk and double cream

4 egg yolks

75g sugar

for the pears

1 William pear

cocoa powder

Separate the eggs and mix the yolks with the stock syrup. Place in a bowl over a pan of simmering water and whisk until it thickens. Remove from heat and allow to cool slightly. In another bowl, melt the chocolate over simmering water. Combine the chocolate in with the yolks and sugar and add the cream. Place into a tray lined with cling film and allow to set. Cut into squares and place in the centre of the plate.

Heat the milk and cream with 4 split vanilla pods. Gently simmer and allow to infuse for 1 hour. Whisk the egg yolks with the sugar and add the milk mixture, slowly cook over a low heat until it thickens to double cream consistency, allow to cool in the fridge.

To serve, place a square of chocolate in the centre of the plate. Slice the pear very finely lengthways (about 5mm thick), dust the tops with cocoa powder and place on top of the chocolate. To complete the dish, spoon a little of the sauce and serve.

CITY CAFE

BRISTOL

Gary Clarke

Piedmontaise peppers with buffalo mozzarella and pesto

serves 4

4 medium red peppers

2 cloves garlic

15ml extra virgin olive oil

2 plum tomatoes, skinned

250g buffalo mozzarella

15g freshly picked basil leaves

for the red pepper dressing

1 medium red pepper

1 plum tomato, skinned

15ml sherry vinegar

150ml extra virgin olive oil

salt and white pepper

for the pesto

75g basil leaves

2 cloves garlic, coarsely chopped

50g pine nuts

300ml extra virgin olive oil

50g Parmesan cheese, grated

salt and black pepper

Cut the peppers in half taking care not to remove the stalk and de-seed. Place on a suitable roasting tray. Pre-set the oven to 170°C/ Gas Mark 5.

To skin the tomatoes, make a cross incision in the tomato and remove the stalk, plunge into boiling water for 10 seconds and re-fresh in cold water and skin. Cut the skinned tomatoes in half and place inside the red peppers. Thinly slice the 2 cloves of garlic and place 1 to 2 pieces on each. Lightly coat the peppers with extra virgin oil and gently season them, place in the oven and roast for 45 minutes, or until soft and lightly coloured. Remove from the oven and allow to cool to room temperature.

For the red pepper dressing, place all the ingredients into a blender except for the sherry vinegar and olive oil. Blend until smooth, then slowly add the olive oil followed by the sherry vinegar, season with salt and pepper and keep until needed.

To make the pesto, place the pine nuts, garlic and half the olive oil in a food processor, mix for 30 seconds. Add the Parmesan, basil leaves and the remaining olive oil, season and mix until smooth. Kept in a jar in the fridge it will last for up to 2 weeks.

To serve, slice the mozzarella allowing 2 slices for each person. Place 2 halves of pepper on each plate with 2 slices of mozzarella and circle with the dressing and pesto. Finish with picked basil.

Steak and ale pudding

serves 4

for the filling

500g chuck steak

100g seasoned flour

1 large onion, sliced

150g field mushrooms, skinned and chopped

300ml Guinness

600ml beef stock

1 bouquet garni

1 bunch watercress

for the suet crust

300g self-raising flour

1 teaspoon baking powder

salt and white pepper

$^1/_2$ teaspoon thyme leaves, chopped

150g beef suet

cold water

To make the filling, start by removing any sinew and excess fat from the steak with a sharp knife and cut into dice. Sprinkle with seasoned flour and brown in batches in a large frying pan. Do not overcrowd the pan. Remove to a large saucepan. Fry the onion until transparent in the same frying pan and de-glaze with the Guinness.

Add the Guinness, onions, mushrooms, the stock and bouquet garni to the meat. Braise for about 3 hours in a moderate oven. Allow to cool and remove any fat from the surface. If the liquor is too thin, strain it into a saucepan and boil to make it thicker. Reserve about 300ml of the liquid for finishing.

For the suet crust, mix all the ingredients together in a bowl and add enough cold water to make a firm dough. Roll out 2/3 of the dough to a thickness of about 5mm. Press into a large pudding basin, allowing a small overlap at the top. Spoon in the filling. Roll out the remaining dough to the same thickness to fit the top of the basin. Place it on top and pinch around the edge, using the overlap to make a good seal. Cover the top of the basin with a piece of foil that has a crease folded along the middle. (This will prevent the foil from splitting when the pudding rises.) Tie with string. Put the basin in a heavy-based pan and add boiling water to the pan to come _ of the way up the sides of the basin. Cover and steam for 3 hours. Remember not to let the pan boil dry - always top up with boiling water.

To serve, put the retained sauce in a pan and heat through. Pour over the pudding, and garnish with watercress.

265

Rhubarb crumble with raspberry syrup

Serves 4

for sable pastry

225g plain flour

120g icing sugar

1 pinch of salt

120g unsalted flour

2 egg yolks

cold milk

for the rhubarb

250g fresh rhubarb

125g caster sugar

1 vanilla pod

75ml water

25g butter

for the crumble

200g plain flour

125g unsalted butter

100g caster sugar

for the raspberry syrup

2 punnets fresh raspberries

50g caster sugar

50ml water

2 vanilla pods

To make sable pastry, combine the flour, icing sugar and salt in a mixing bowl with a wooden spoon and rub in the butter. Mix in the egg yolks to make a good dough consistency. Add milk if necessary. This is a very delicate pastry. Chill for an hour, or more and use as required.

Peel the rhubarb and chop thoroughly, discarding any flowers. Melt the butter over a low heat, add the rhubarb, sugar, vanilla and water and stew until all the water has evaporated. Remove from the heat and allow to cool to room temperature. Line the individual tartlet moulds with pastry and bake blind at 180°C/Gas Mark 6, until light golden. Allow to cool do not remove from the case.

Fill the tartlet case with the rhubarb mixture until level, top with the crumble mixture and bake at 200°C/ Gas Mark 7, until golden brown, leave to rest for about 8 minutes.

For the crumble, melt the butter over a low heat. Mix the sugar and flour together. Make a well in the centre and pour in the melted butter. Allow to cool slightly, then rub in the butter with a wooden spoon.

To make the raspberry syrup, place the raspberries in a bowl with the water, add the seeds from the split vanilla pod and the sugar. Cover and set aside for 1 hour. Blend in a food processor until smooth and strain to remove any seeds.

To serve, remove the crumble from the case place a ball of vanilla ice cream on the top of the crumble, spoon the sauce around the outside to a decorative manner, then place the retained vanilla pod on top of vanilla ice cream and serve.

TYLNEY HALL

Steven Hine

Dressed crab with gazpacho

serves 4

125g fresh white crab meat

2 teaspoons mayonnaise

1 ripe avocado, peeled and stoned

juice of $1/2$ lime

a pinch of chilli powder or a few drops of Tabasco sauce

4 tablespoons soured cream

salt and freshly ground black pepper

For the gazpacho

300g plum tomatoes, roughly chopped

100g cucumber, peeled, deseeded and roughly chopped

100g red peppers, roughly chopped

$1/2$ bunch of basil, roughly chopped

4 teaspoons white wine vinegar

4 teaspoons caster sugar

First make the gazpacho. Mix all the ingredients together in a bowl, then cover and leave to marinate in the fridge overnight. The next day, purée the mixture with a little water in a food processor or blender. Pass through a fine sieve and season to taste, then chill thoroughly.

Mix the crab meat and mayonnaise together, season and then place in the fridge. Purée half the avocado in a blender with the lime juice and chilli or Tabasco. Cut the remaining avocado into small dice and fold it into the purée.

Place a plain 5cm pastry cutter in the centre of a soup plate and fill it three-quarters full with the crab mixture. Top it up with the avocado mixture, then carefully remove the cutter. Repeat on 3 more soup plates. Place a spoonful of soured cream on top of each avocado and crab gâteau, then slow pour the gazpacho around the edge. Serve within an hour.

Pan-fried sea bass with steamed mussels and summer vegetables

serves 4

250ml fish stock

500g mussels, well scrubbed
(discard any open ones that won't
close when pressed lightly)

4 x 200g sea bass fillets

2 tablespoons olive oil

2 tablespoons white wine

4 tablespoons double cream

110g chilled unsalted butter,
cut into small cubes

salt and freshly ground black pepper

For the summer vegetables:

a bunch of baby carrots

8 asparagus spears

a bunch of baby fennel

1 small courgette, cut into batons

4 baby leeks

6 button onions or shallots

25g butter

Trim all the vegetables, peeling the onions or shallots. Cook them separately in boiling salted water until just tender, then drain. Refresh under cold running water and set aside.

Heat a few tablespoons of the fish stock in a large pan, add the mussels, then cover tightly and cook for 2-3 minutes, shaking the pan occasionally, until the mussels have opened. Strain through a fine sieve and set the mussels aside, reserving the strained juices.

Season the bass fillets. Heat the oil in a large, heavy-based frying pan, add the bass, skin-side down, and cook for about 4 minutes, until the skin is golden brown. Turn and cook for about 4 minutes longer, until the bass is just done. Remove from the heat and keep warm.

To make the sauce, put the remaining fish stock and the white wine in a pan and boil until reduced by half. Add the strained mussel cooking liquid and the double cream and simmer until reduced by about a third. Remove from the heat and whisk in the butter a few cubes at a time. Keep warm.

Reheat all the vegetables in the butter, then divide them between 4 serving plates. Place the bass fillets on top, skin-side up, and surround with the steamed mussels. Pour the sauce around the edge, taking care not to pour it over the bass, as it will spoil the crisp skin.

Modern baked Alaska with fruit salad and mango coulis

serves 4

90g mixed soft fruit, finely diced
(eg strawberries, raspberries,
pineapple, mango, papaya, melon)

250ml vanilla ice-cream
(or flavour of your choice)

90ml mango coulis
(a good-quality bought one is fine)

4 sprigs of mint

For the tuiles:

50g unsalted butter

50g icing sugar

1 egg white, lightly beaten

45g plain flour

a drop of vanilla extract

For the Italian meringue:

110g caster sugar

90ml water

3 egg whites

To make the tuiles, cream the butter and icing sugar together until light, then gradually add the beaten egg white. Sift in the flour and fold in with the vanilla extract.

Line a large baking sheet with baking parchment and draw four 16 x 8cm rectangles on the paper. Fill them with the mixture, spreading it out with a palette knife. Bake in an oven preheated to 180°C/Gas Mark 4 for 3-4 minutes, until golden, then remove from the oven and leave to cool for a couple of minutes. While they are still warm and pliable, roll each tuile into an open cylindrical shape, either by hand or shaping it round a wooden rolling pin. Leave to cool completely.

For the meringue, place 90g of the sugar in a heavy-based pan with the water, bring slowly to the boil until the sugar has dissolved, then boil for about 5 minutes or until the mixture reaches 120°C on a sugar thermometer. Meanwhile, using an electric beater, whisk the egg whites with the remaining sugar until they form stiff peaks. Trickle in the boiled sugar syrup, whisking constantly, then continue to whisk until the meringue is cold. It is now ready for use or can be stored in the fridge until required.

To assemble the dessert, place a tuile cylinder on each serving plate and place a spoonful of the mixed soft fruit inside it. Fill with ice-cream and pipe the meringue on top. Glaze under a hot grill for a few seconds, until the meringue is golden brown. Quickly spoon the rest of the fruit salad and the mango coulis over it, decorate with the mint and serve immediately.

THE MANSION HOUSE

Gerry Godden

Terrine of mackerel and rocket mash with seared scallops and tomato relish

serves 10

3 x 500g mackerel, filleted and pinned

6 baking potatoes

2 potatoes, peeled and sliced very thinly

500g rocket, deep-fried

20 scallops, cleaned and roes removed

salt and freshly ground pepper

juice of 1 lemon

melted butter

for the tomato relish

500g ripe tomatoes, skinned

50g red pepper, de-seeded and finely chopped

3 shallots, finely chopped

50g celery, chopped

75ml vinegar

1 x 5ml teaspoon mustard seeds, crushed

1 x 25ml teaspoon cayenne pepper

50g sugar

Line a 10" x 3" terrine with cling film. Dip the sliced potatoes into the melted butter and place onto baking trays lined with non-stick baking mats. Cook in a medium oven until soft but not coloured. Remove from the oven and line the terrine with the potato slices. Bake the potatoes until cooked, cut in half, scoop out the potato, mash, season and add the deep fried rocket and lemon juice.

Season the mackerel, brush with olive oil and grill until just cooked.

Put a layer of the rocket mash into the bottom of the terrine about 1/2" deep, then lay 3 mackerel fillets on top overlapping the thinner ends. Continue layering with mash and mackerel and top with the overlapping potato slices. Cover with cling film, press down and chill well before serving.

To make the tomato relish, roughly chop the tomatoes and put them into a thick-bottomed pan with the shallots, celery and red pepper. Cook for 10 minutes, add the vinegar, mustard, cayenne pepper, sugar and cook for at least 30 minutes until the relish is thick and pulpy. Allow to cool.

To serve, place a slice of terrine on a plate, garnish with mixed leaves, a quenelle of tomato relish and finish with 2 seared scallops.

Breast of Gressingham duck
with a sun-dried sweet and sour cherry spring roll

serves 4

4 180g-200g Gressingham duck breasts

1 carrot, peeled and cut into small dice and cooked in salted water until just tender

50g sun-dried sweet and sour cherries, chopped and soaked in cold water

4 shallots, chopped

1 clove garlic, chopped

1 teaspoon rosemary, finely chopped

2 bunches baby turnips, cleaned and cooked

4 x 8" square, egg-roll/spring roll wrappers (available from a good delicatessen)

1 egg white, beaten with a little water

100ml port

200ml red wine

500ml brown chicken stock

salt and freshly ground pepper

for the glazed button onions

12 button onions, peeled

1 knob of butter

1 sprig of rosemary

for the chicken cream

2 shallots, sliced

100ml Vermouth

200ml light chicken stock

150ml whipping cream

To make the sauce, fry the shallots and garlic in a little oil until golden. Add the rosemary, wine and port, stirring to de-glaze the pan. Reduce the liquid by half, then add the chicken stock and reduce again by half. Season and strain through a fine sieve into a clean pan.

Remove each end of the duck breast to leave 4 nice pieces of duck breast almost square shaped. Remove the fat from the duck ends and finely chop the meat. Put into a bowl and mix in the carrot, rosemary and cherries. Season with salt and pepper. Working with 1 spring roll wrapper at a time, apply beaten egg white with a pastry brush around the edge of the wrapper. Place a mound of filling in the centre, fold 1 corner over the filling, roll halfway then fold in the opposing corners and continue to roll to make a firm cylinder.

For the glazed onions, heat a pan with a lid and add the butter, shallots, rosemary and a tablespoon of water. Replace the lid to cook the onions for 5 minutes then remove, evaporate the liquid and glaze the onions.

For the chicken cream, soften the shallots in a little oil without colour. Add the Vermouth and reduce by half. Add the stock and reduce by half again. Add the cream, bring to the boil, season and strain through a fine sieve into a clean pan.

Heat a heavy based frying pan and cook the duck breast skin-side down for about 10 minutes until very crisp. Then turn over and cook for a further 2 minutes. Remove from the pan and allow to rest. Fry the spring rolls until golden and crisp, drain onto kitchen paper. Warm the turnips, onions and the sauces.

To serve, place the duck on the 4 serving plates. Cut the spring rolls straight at one end and on a slant at the other and sit next to the duck. Pour a small amount of red wine sauce onto the plate and spoon the turnips and onions around. Froth the chicken cream and finish the dish.

Lemon meringue

serves 4

for the sable pastry

75g butter

75g icing sugar

160g flour

1 egg, beaten

for the lemon curd

juice and zest of 2 lemons

2 whole eggs

2 egg yolks (keep the whites for the meringue)

100g caster sugar

150ml double cream

for the meringue

2 egg whites at room temperature

100g caster sugar

for the lemon curd ice cream

$^1/_2$ of the above lemon curd

2 tablespoons Greek yoghurt

1 tablespoon cream

for the raspberry coulis

200g raspberries

juice of $^1/_2$ lemon

100ml stock syrup

To make the pastry, cream the butter and icing sugar together until white and add the egg. Fold in the flour, knead to a dough and refrigerate for at least 2 hours.

Roll out onto a lightly floured surface and line 4 x 5cm tartlet moulds. Line with cling film and baking beans and bake blind for 8-10 minutes. Remove the beans and return to the oven for a further 2-4 minutes and cool.

To make the lemon curd, whisk the egg yolks in a bowl over hot water. Add the sugar until it thickens and doubles in volume. Add the lemon juice, zest and cream, whisking continuously over the water until the mixture thickens.

For the meringues, put the egg whites into a very clean electric mixer. Beat the egg whites into soft peaks. Gradually add the sugar a tablespoon at a time and continue whisking into firm peaks. Using a star nozzle, pipe out 8-10 swan shaped bodies. Using a small plain nozzle, pipe out 10 -12 'S' shaped swan heads. Place in a very low oven and dry/cook out.

To make the ice cream, churn all the ingredients in an ice cream machine until frozen.

For the coulis, purée the fresh or frozen raspberries with the juices of half a lemon with the stock syrup and sieve to remove the seeds.

To serve, fill the tart with lemon curd, dust with icing sugar and caramelise with a blowtorch. Place onto a plate. Sandwich a ball of lemon curd ice cream between 2 swan bodies and attach the swan head and sit on the plate. Zigzag the raspberry coulis behind the swan and serve.

THE KITCHENS

AMBERLEY CASTLE

Amberley, nr Arundel, West Sussex BN18 9ND
Tel: +44 (0)1798 831992   Fax: +44 (0)1798 831998
E mail: info@amberleycastle.co.uk
16

ASHDOWN PARK

Wych Cross, Forest Row, East Sussex RH18 5JR
Tel: +44 (0)1342 824988   Fax: +44 (0)1342 826206
E mail: sales@ashdownpark.com
125

THE ATLANTIC HOTEL

Le Mont de la Pulente, St Brelade, Jersey JE3 8HE
Tel: +44 (0)1534 744101   Fax: +44 (0)1534 744102
E mail: info@theatlantichotel.com
191

BINDON
COUNTRY HOUSE HOTEL

Langford Budville, Wellington, Somerset TA21 0RU
Tel: +44 (0)1823 400070   Fax: +44 (0)1823 400071
E mail: stay@bindon.com
149

BLAKES HOTEL

33 Roland Gardens, London SW7 3PF
Tel: +44 (0)20 7370 6701   Fax: +44 (0)20 7373 0442
E mail: blakes@easynet.co.uk
154

CALLOW HALL

Mappleton, Ashbourne, Derbyshire DE6 2AA
Tel: +44 (0)1335 300900   Fax: +44 (0)1335 300512
E mail: reservations@callowhall.co.uk
107

CASHEL PALACE HOTEL

Main Street, Cashel, Co Tipperary
Tel: +353 (0)62 62707   Fax: +353 (0)62 61521
E mail: reception@cashel-palace.ie
120

CHARLTON HOUSE
AND THE MULBERRY RESTAURANT

Charlton Road, Shepton Mallet, nr Bath, Somerset BA4 4PR
Tel: +44 (0)1749 342008   Fax: +44 (0)1749 346362
E-mail: enquiry@charltonhouse.com
233

CHEWTON GLEN

New Milton, Hampshire BH25 6QS
Tel: +44 (0)1425 275341   Fax: +44 (0)1425 272310
E mail: reservations@chewtonglen.com
36

CHILSTON PARK HOTEL

Sandway, Lenham, Nr Maidstone, Kent ME17 2BE
Tel: +44 (0)1622 859803 Fax: +44 (0)1622 858588
E mail: chilstonpark@arcadianhotels.co.uk
200

CITY CAFE
BIRMINGHAM

Brindveyrlace, Birmingham B1 2HW
Tel: 0121 6336300   Fax: 0161 6431005
E mail: cityinn@reservations.com
50

CITY CAFE
BRISTOL

Temple Rose Street, Bristol BS1 6BF
Tel: 0117 9251001   Fax: 0117 9074116
E mail: cityinn@reservations.com
262

CITY CAFE
GLASGOW

Finnieston Quay, Glasgow G3 8HN
Tel: 0141 2271010   Fax: 0141 2482754
E mail: cityinn@reservations.com
84

CRATHORNE HALL

Crathorne, Yarm, North Yorkshire TS15 0AR
Tel: +44 (0)1642 700398   Fax: +44 (0)1642 700814
E mail: crathorne@arcadianhotels.co.uk
102

CREWE HALL

Weston Road, Crewe, Cheshire CW1 6UZ
Tel: +44 (0)1270 253333   Fax: +44 (0)1270 253322
E mail: information@crewehall.co.uk

111

DANESFIELD HOUSE
HOTEL & SPA

Henley Road, Marlow, Buckinghamshire SL7 2EY
Tel: +44 (0)1628 891010   Fax: +44 (0)1628 890408
E mail: sales@danesfieldhouse.co.uk

40

THE DEVONSHIRE ARMS

Bolton Abbey, Skipton, N Yorkshire BD23 6AJ
Tel: +44(0)1756 710441   Fax: +44 (0)1756 710564
E mail: sales@thedevonshirearms.co.uk

163

DROMOLAND CASTLE

Newmarket-on-Fergus, Co Clare
Tel: +353 (0)61 368144   Fax: +353 (0)61 363355
E mail: sales@dromoland.ie

21

ETTINGTON PARK HOTEL

Alderminster, Stratford upon Avon, Warks CV37 8BU
Tel: +44 (0)1789 450123   Fax: +44 (0)1789 450472
E mail: ettington@arcadianhotels.co.uk

79

FAIRYHILL

Reynoldston, Gower, Swansea SA3 1BS
Tel: 01792 390139   Fax: 01792 391358
E mail: postbox@fairyhill.net

55

THE GIBBON BRIDGE HOTEL

near Chipping, Forest of Bowland, Preston, Lancs PR3 2TQ
Tel: +44 (0)1995 61456   Fax: +44 (0)1995 61277
E-mail: reception@gibbon-bridge.co.uk

116

THE GRAND HOTEL

King Edward's Parade, Eastbourne, East Sussex BN21 4EQ
Tel: +44 (0)1323 412345   Fax: +44 (0)1323 412233
E mail: reservations@grandeastbourne.com

229

HOLBROOK HOUSE & SPA

Wincanton, Somerset BA9 8BS
tel: 01963 32377   Fax01963 32681
enquiries@holbrookhouse.co.uk

31

THE HORN OF PLENTY

Gulworthy, Tavistock, Devon PL19 8JD
Tel: +44 (0)1822 832528   Fax: +44 (0)1822 832528
E mail: enquiries@thehornofplenty.co.uk

93

KINNAIRD

Kinnaird Estate, By Dunkeld, Perthshire PH8 0LB
Tel: +44 (0)1796 482440   Fax: +44 (0)1796 482289
E mail: enquiry@kinnairdestate.com

16

LANGSHOTT MANOR

Langshott, near Gatwick, Surrey RH6 9LN
Tel: +44 (0)1293 786680   Fax: +44 (0)1293 783905
E mail: admin@langshottmanor.com

205

LONGUEVILLE MANOR

St Saviour, Jersey, Channel Islands JE2 7WF
Tel: +44 (0)1534 725501   Fax: +44 (0)1534 731613
E mail: longman@itl.net

89

THE LOWRY HOTEL

50 Dearmons Place, Chapel Wharf, Salford,
Manchester M3 5LH
Tel: 0161 8274000   Fax: 0161 827 4001
Email: enquiries@thelowryhotel.com

26

MALLORY COURT

Harbury Lane, Bishops Tachbrook
Leamington Spa CV33 9QB
Tel: +44 (0)1926 330214   Fax: +44 (0)1926 451714
E mail: reception@mallory.co.uk
195

THE MANSION HOUSE

Thames Street, Poole, Dorset BH15 1JN
Tel: +44 (0)1202 685666   Fax: +44 (0)1202 665709
E mail: enquiries@themansionhouse.co.uk
271

THE MARCLIFFE AT PITFODELS

North Deeside Road, Aberdeen AB15 9YA
Tel: +44 (0)1224 861000   Fax: +44 (0)1224 868860
E mail: enquiries@marcliffe.com
60

MATFEN HALL

Matfen, Northumberland NE20 0RH
Tel: 01661 886500   Fax: 01661 886055
E mail: info@matfenhall.com
215

MORSTON HALL
HOTEL & RESTAURANT

Morston, Holt, Norfolk NR25 7AA
Tel: 01263 741041   Fax: 01263 740419
E mail: reception@morstonhall.com
74

NEW HALL

Walmley Road, Royal Sutton Coldfield
West Midlands B76 1QX
Tel: +44 (0)121 378 2442   Fax: +44 (0)121 378 4637
E mail: new.hall@thistle.co.uk
140

NEWICK PARK

Newick, East Sussex BN8 4SB
Tel: 01825 723633   Fax: 01825 723969
E mail: bookings@newickpark.co.uk
158

NUTFIELD PRIORY

Nutfield, Nr Redhill, Surrey RH1 4EL
Tel: 01737 824400   Fax: 01737 823321
E mail: nutpriory@aol.com
130

NUTHURST GRANGE
COUNTRY HOUSE

Nuthurst Grange Lane, Hockley Heath
West Midlands B94 5NL
Tel: 01564 783972   Fax: 01564 783919
E mail: info@nuthurst-grange.co.uk
70

THE OLD BELL AT MALMESBURY

Abbey Row, Malmesbury, Wiltshire SN16 0AG
Tel: +44 (0)1666 822344   Fax: +44 (0)1666 825145
E mail: info@oldbellhotel.com
257

THE PEAT INN

by Cupar, Fife KY15 5LH
Tel: 01334-840206   Fax: 01334-840530
E mail: reception@thepeatinn.co.uk
135

PORTMARNOCK HOTEL
& GOLF LINKS

Strand Road, Portmarnock, Co Dublin
Tel: +353 (0)1 846 0611   Fax: +353 (0)1 846 2442
E mail: marketing@portmarnock.com
144

LE POUSSIN AT PARKHILL

Beaulieu Road, Lyndhurst, Hampshire SO43 7FZ
Tel: +44 (0)2380 282944   Fax: +44 (0)2380 283268
E mail: sales@lepoussinatparkhill.co.uk
182

THE PRIEST HOUSE
ON THE RIVER

Kings Mills, Castle Donington, Derby DE74 2RR
Tel: +44 (0)1332 810649   Fax: +44 (0)1332 811141
E mail: priesthouse@arcadianhotels.co.uk
172

THE PRIORY BAY HOTEL

Priory Drive, Seaview, Isle of Wight PO34 5BU
Tel: +44 (0)1983 613146   Fax: +44 (0)1983 616539
E mail: reception@priorybay.co.uk
219

THE QUEENSBERRY

Russel Street, Bath BA1 2QF
Tel: +44 (0)1225 447928   Fax: +44 (0)1225 446065
E mail: queensberry@dial.pipex.com
45

RIBER HALL

Riber, Matlock, Derbyshire DE4 5JU
Tel: +44 (0)1629 582795   Fax: +44 (0)1629 580475
E mail: info@riber-hall.co.uk
177

THE SAVOY

The Strand, London WC2R 0EU
Tel 020 74202329   Fax: 020 7240 6040
E mail: info@the-savoy.co.uk
10

SHARROW BAY
COUNTRY HOUSE HOTEL

Lake Ullswater, Howtown, Penrith, Cumbria CA10 2LZ
Tel: +44 (0)17684 86301   Fax: +44 (0)17684 86349
E Mail: enquiries@sharrow-bay.com
186

SHEEN FALLS LODGE

Kenmare, Co Kerry
Tel: +353 (0)64 41600   Fax: +353 (0)64 41386
E mail: info@sheenfallslodge.ie
210

STOKE PARK CLUB

Park Road, Stoke Poges, Buckinghamshire SL2 4PG
Tel: +44 (0)1753 717171   Fax: +44 (0)1753 717181
E mail: info@stokeparkclub.com
224

THE SWAN HOTEL

Bibury, Gloucestershire GL7 5NW
Tel: +44 (0)1285 740695   Fax: +44 (0)1285 740473
E mail: swanhot1@swanhotel-cotswolds.co.uk
65

STUDLEY PRIORY

Horton Hill, Horton-Cum-Studley, Oxford OX33 1AZ
Tel: 01865 351203   Fax: 01865 351613
E mail: res@studley-priory.co.uk
238

THATCHED COTTAGE
HOTEL & RESTAURANT

16 Brookley Road, Brockenhurst, Hampshire SO42 7RR
Tel: +44 (0)1590 623090   Fax: +44 (0)1590 623479
E mail: sales@thatchedcottage.co.uk
247

TYLNEY HALL

Rotherwick, Hook, Hampshire RG27 9AZ
Tel: +44 (0)1256 764881   Fax: +44 (0)1256 768141
E mail: sales@tylneyhall.com
267

WATERFORD CASTLE

The Island, Ballinakill, Waterford
Tel: +353 (0)51 878203   Fax: +353 (0)51 879316
E mail: info@waterfordcastle.com
243

WINTERINGHAM FIELDS

Winteringham, North Lincolnshire DN15 9PF
Tel: +44 (0)1724 733096   Fax: +44 (0)1724 733898
E mail: wintfields@aol.com
98

WOOD NORTON HALL

Wood Norton, Evesham, Worcestershire WR11 4YB
Tel: +44 (0)1386 420007   Fax: +44 (0)1386 420679
E mail: woodnorton.hall@bbc.co.uk
252

INDEX OF RECIPES

THE JEWEL IN THE CROWN

Château Mouton Rothschild – a claret with personality, just like its owner, says Serena Sutcliffe, MW.

Premier Cru status in any region is a huge responsibility, but owning a First Growth Château in Bordeaux must be somewhat like snaffling three Michelin stars – the only way to go is down! Standards have to be kept high and scrutiny is constant, but at least the Bordeaux Château classification has not been reviewed since 1855. The long-awaited and much-deserved elevation of Château Mouton Rothschild to Premier Cru status came in 1973 – and this has been the only change.

Mouton, as it is affectionately known, is, with Lafite and Latour, one of three Premiers Crus in Pauillac. This must make it the most majestic appellation in Bordeaux's Médoc region. Mouton has a special, hugely showy character – deep, opulent and full of cassis fruit. Its spicy, blackcurrant bouquet comes surging out of the glass and the huge, aromatic flavour is all-enveloping – claret with personality, like its owner, Baroness Philippine de Rothschild.

I have observed that people tend to look like their pets, but I am also sure of the link between people and their wines. Philippine de Rothschild is exuberance itself. Before succeeding her father, she was a leading actress in Paris, which, amazingly enough, can help in promoting a superb wine. A First Growth Château owner is required to travel all over the world to present the wine and, while it 'speaks for itself' in the glass, an entertaining and informative châtelaine will forever fix the taste in your mind.

Château Mouton Rothschild is the jewel in a crown of properties and joint ventures that make impressive reading. Two other classed growths, Château d'Armailhac and Clerc Milon, belong to the family, and then there is a 100-hectare estate in the Languedoc (the most up-and-coming quality region in France), the joint venture with Robert Mondavi in California, Opus One, as well as Almaviva in Chile, the ubiquitous Mouton Cadet and a mass of Bordeaux appellation wines and vins de pays varietals from the Pays d'Oc. You cannot forget your lines with such a stable full of stars.

The actual Château at Mouton is small – the emphasis is on the vineyards and cellars. First Growth vines receive tender loving care throughout the year, but I think the way the top leaves are trimmed in summer (called rognage in French) gives an image of perfect gardening. Mouton is an 80 per cent

Cabernet Sauvignon-dominated wine, which, together with the gravelly soil, contributes to the black fruit profile of the taste. Handpicking is done by a team of hundreds, and the wine is given a long fermentation in oak vats and matured in 100 per cent new oak barrels. Only such a dense, powerful wine as a Bordeaux First Growth can take such an input of new oak tannins, but Mouton simply laps it up.

The result is a wine of stunning impact and great longevity. A few years ago, I led a memorable tasting, and even more memorable dinner, when we went back to the 1924 vintage. Everything was in magnum, the optimum size if you wish to keep wine for decades. We had all the trophy vintages, such as 1945, 1961 and 1982, as well as other gems such as the 1949, 1953, 1955 and 1962. Among younger vintages, the 1985 is superb and, as yet, undervalued, while the 1986 is a giant, requiring patience. The trio of 1988, 1989 and 1990 promises hedonistic pleasure on a grand scale, while I would drink a lighter vintage, like 1993 or 1997, relatively young. Both 1995 and 1996 will be 'keepers', and the splendid 1998 has only just been bottled.

As with so many committed wine people, Philippine de Rothschild is also a passionate art lover, evinced both in the additions to the wine and art museum at Mouton and in the eclectic yearly commissioning of the artists who design the labels. This brilliant idea has been much emulated but never equalled – the lure of receiving some Mouton from the label's vintage as a thank you clearly brings in the world's most exciting daubers, although even they cannot control the weather in 'their' year!

Naturally, Mouton is not my daily tipple, but I savour every drop that comes my way. At a recent, joyous Sunday lunch at the Château, we were lucky enough to drink the legendary 1959, a profound, multi-dimensional wine of great, thick, ripe appeal. And, at a country weekend in the English countryside last summer, we were downing Mouton's intriguing white wine, Aile d'Argent, named after a fairy story that Baron Philippe used to tell his daughter, Philippine, when she was a child.

That is what a family Château is all about – shared memories and traditions, as well as motivation, to hand over something precious to future generations.

Distinction
TO YOUR DOOR

SEVEN SUPERB PUBLICATIONS

1 copy of Distinction 2002:
the supreme hardback directory,
containing an unrivalled selection
of the United Kingdom & Ireland's finest hotels
with information on rates and facilities.

2 issues of Distinction – the Magazine:
published in May and October each year,
a beautifully produced colour magazine
filled with hotel features, recipes, lifestyle editorial,
and updated information on Distinction's hotels.

May & October 2002

4 mailings of Distinction News:
a quarterly newsletter with fabulous added value deals for subscribers.
From champagne on arrival to free nights, from discounts on room rates
to special packages: whether you are seeking a romantic break
or the venue for a special event,
Distinction News is an inspiring collection of exclusive offers.

Mar/Jun/Sep/Dec 2002

ANNUAL SUBSCRIPTION: ONLY £37.50

CONTACT PTARMIGAN PUBLISHING

01380 728700